Nonprofit Finance:
A Practical Guide

Sheila Shanker, CPA

Published by Sheila Shanker - U.S.A. 2015

ISBN: 150599540X
ISBN-13: 978-1505995404

To my husband, Ud Shanker, with love.

Nonprofit Finance: A Practical Guide

CONTENTS

1

Introduction

T his book provides a detailed overview of the major nonprofit areas for persons interested in the fiscal operations of an organization, such as financial statements, accounting, grant management, internal controls and tax issues.

I recommend this publication as a useful, practical resource for any new controller, manager, board member, or CFO working in the nonprofit sector. Maybe you have questions regarding operations or specific accounting issues, such as:

- Is the nonprofit tax-exempt?
- What are "funds" or "net assets"?
- What is a "release of net assets"?
- What is a Statement of Position?
- What is a Statement of Activities?
- What are grant costs?

This book answers these questions and others you may have in the back of your mind regarding the nonprofit sector. Some chapters are more technical than others, so if you are not accounting-oriented, you may still understand the concepts. Additionally, terminology and vocabulary are explained with numerous examples to clarify typical nonprofit models of operation, taxes, and financial reporting.

Examples of letters, forms, and reports pertinent to the nonprofit world are presented along with vignettes of my own experiences and recommendations, giving the material a different perspective than a purely academic or technical approach.

Each chapter covers an important topic within the nonprofit world, combining theory and practical information to make the issues clear and simple to understand.

The material is based on IRS, Financial Accounting Standards Board (FASB), and other government publications, including the "Super Circular," the new federal grant guide. Please note that, like everything in life, things change, and you must keep up with the modifications in the law and accounting regulations.

I hope you find this book an informative and valuable resource to better understand and appreciate the nonprofit world.

2

Fundamentals of Accounting

"Wikipedia is a non-profit. It was either the dumbest thing I ever did or the smartest thing I ever did. Communities can build amazing things, but you have to be part of that community, and you cannot abuse them. You have to be very respectful of what their needs are."

Jimmy Wales, founder of Wikipedia (Keynote Speech, SXSW 2006)

Wikipedia is indeed one of the thousands of nonprofits based in the U.S. providing goods/services to many communities. Clearly, the nonprofit sector is not a new fad, as the U.S. has a long history of philanthropy. One of the first organized campaigns for donations was the "United Thank Offering," created by the Episcopal Church in 1889. Christmas Seals was founded in the early 1900s due to the spread of tuberculosis and other lung diseases. Other known charities, such as the Boy Scouts, National Association for the Advancement of Colored People, and Goodwill, were created between 1909 and 1913.

The nonprofit sector is growing, with about 962,000 public charities in the U.S. in 2014. Nonprofits were also responsible for 9.2% of all salaries paid in the U.S. in 2010, according to the National Center for Charitable Statistics.

The largest nonprofit organization is the Bill and Melinda Gates Foundation, with an endowment of about $40 billion, making it the biggest in the world. This foundation has committed billions of dollars in grants since its inception to fund various global programs.

Characteristics of Nonprofits

Nonprofits can be museums, social agencies, or humanitarian services. They are not in business to make a profit—they are in business to serve a community with goods and services. For instance, the Arthritis Foundation's goal is to help people with arthritis and their families. The Red Cross assists people when disaster strikes.

Nonprofit organizations have the unique status of possessing no "real" ownership. They retain boards of directors, but not owners per se. The idea is that nonprofits are actually owned by a community or members they serve.

✓ **A nonprofit organization is a business unable to hold or distribute profits like a "for-profit" organization.**

Nonprofit organizations cannot distribute earnings, issue, or sell stock/shares. As it can be expected, since nonprofits cannot pay dividends on any earnings, and have no owners, one cannot "invest" in nonprofit organizations the same way that one can in a business. A person or business can promote certain programs by donating to a nonprofit, but the expectation of getting a return on investment does not exist.

Revenue streams for nonprofits are quite different from for-profits that get their revenue from goods and services sold at a profit. In contrast, nonprofit revenues typically come from fundraising events and:

- Governments
- Foundations
- Businesses
- Individual donors
- Trusts
- Estates

When organizations hold fundraising events, they often mention large donors or "patrons" in their literature and brochures, providing donors with visibility and goodwill in the community. Some businesses, such as large accounting firms, offer employees as volunteers to increase their prominence locally. Even though the profit motive is not present, reputable nonprofits have proper cash flows and measures in place to function effectively.

Nonprofit organizations are also known as "charities," "exempt organizations," or even "NPOs." They can be large or small. Several prominent hospitals and universities like Kaiser Permanente and UCLA are set up as nonprofits. Other well-known nonprofits are the Better Business Bureau, Carnegie Corporation of New York, and the New York State Society of CPAs.

If a nonprofit organization has a website, you can easily recognize it by the ".org" at the end of the website address. With educational institutions, you may see the ".edu" instead. However, this is not always the case—I know of a few nonprofits that use ".com" as part of their email addresses.

People may think of nonprofits as an extended arm of government in the sense that many receive government funding to supply services that "big government" cannot provide. However, nonprofits are not a part of the government; they are separate entities that may receive government funding, although this is not mandatory.

Nonprofits may receive money for various purposes. Some nonprofits conduct or support medical research, and they receive funds from government organizations, such as NIH (National Institutes of Health), family trusts, or foundations interested in specific illnesses. Grants and gifts have different compliance issues, making this area quite challenging.

Many nonprofits are based in the U.S. but operate worldwide, such as the Red Cross, which conducts a lot of its charitable work outside the U.S. Employees of such large organizations are very knowledgeable about foreign laws, because operations of international nonprofits can be quite complex.

I have witnessed the case of a charity worker jailed in Africa, prompting action from the U.S. managers. It was challenging, to say the least. The charity worker was released, and the case ended up well because officials knew how to handle the situation. So some nonprofits can be involved in dangerous situations, highlighting the need for knowledgeable staff.

Outside the U.S., the United Kingdom recognizes nonprofits as "charities." These must be registered with the U.K. Charity Commission. Some countries call nonprofits "NGOs," nongovernmental organizations. The idea is the same—these organizations are not governmental, but receive funding from governments and other entities to conduct tasks relevant to their missions.

Since funding is limited in many organizations, volunteering is a vital characteristic of nonprofits. People volunteer for all kinds of jobs, from administrative assistants to presidents. In fact, some organizations run on volunteers alone. Managing volunteers can be challenging, but done right, it can greatly benefit the organization.

One of my experiences with volunteers happened when I was a controller at a nonprofit. A developmentally disabled woman used to help with Accounts Payable filing. She was a valuable member of the department and felt good about having something important to do. The Accounts Payable accountant was happy to receive the volunteer assistance. So, volunteers can be a big help when managed properly.

Volunteers can show up any place within an organization's structure, including as presidents and board members. Volunteers may not be paid, but they are usually committed to the organization's mission and are instrumental in steering programs and administrative processes.

Tax-Exempt Status

In the U.S., a nonprofit organization is a business entity that has received an exemption from the IRS, so it does not pay income taxes. However, most nonprofits are required to file reports about their activities, even though they are not required to pay income taxes.

Nonprofits/tax-exempt organizations come in a wide variety of code sections that relate to specific activities. For example, chambers of commerce can become tax-exempt under Section 501(c)(6), not 501(c)(3). Following is a list of the code sections related to tax-exemption options.

501(c)(1)	Corporations created by Congress, such as Federal Credit Unions
501(c)(2)	Title-holding corporations for exempt organizations. Limited to own real estate and collect funds
501(c)(3)	**Nonprofit, religious, and educational organizations, including many hospitals. The 501(c)(3) is the focus of this publication.**
501(c)(4)	Various political education organizations
501(c)(5)	Labor unions and agriculture
501(c)(6)	Business league and chamber of commerce organizations
501(c)(7)	Recreational club organizations
501(c)(8)	Fraternal beneficiary societies
501(c)(9)	Voluntary employee beneficiary associations
501(c)(10)	Fraternal lodge societies
501(c)(11)	Teachers' retirement fund associations
501(c)(12)	Local benevolent life insurance associations, mutual irrigation, telephone companies, and like organizations
501(c)(13)	Cemetery companies
501(c)(14)	Credit unions
501(c)(15)	Mutual insurance companies
501(c)(16)	Corporations organized to finance crop operations
501(c)(17)	Employees' associations
501(c)(18)	Employee-funded pension trusts created before June 25, 1959
501(c)(19)	Veterans' organizations
501(c)(20)	Group legal services plan organizations
501(c)(21)	Black lung benefit trusts
501(c)(22)	Withdrawal liability payment fund
501(c)(23)	Veterans' organizations created before 1880
501(c)(24)	Section 4049 ERISA Trusts
501(c)(25)	Title-holding corporations for qualified exempt organizations
501(c)(26)	State-sponsored high-risk health coverage organizations
501(c)(27)	State-sponsored workers' compensation reinsurance organizations
501(c)(28)	National railroad retirement investment trust

All organizations mentioned are tax-exempt for different reasons. A chamber of commerce, for instance, is formed to support local businesses, while a food bank is created to help the poor. These nonprofits are tax-exempt, even if they differ in mission and objectives.

The focus of this publication relates to organizations that are tax-exempt under 501(c)(3). Whenever a "nonprofit" or "nonprofit organization" is mentioned, assume we are dealing with a 501(c)(3) organization.

Section 501(c)(3) lists the following exempt purposes:

- Charitable
- Educational
- Religious
- Scientific
- Literary
- Public safety testing
- Cruelty prevention to children and animals
- Support of sports competitions

The IRS keeps an "Exempt Organizations Business Master File" that identifies nonprofits exempted under 501(c)(3) and other sections. Many grantors will only accept grant applications from organizations in this list.

Form 1023

To become an exempt organization under Section 501(c)(3), a nonprofit generally files the Form 1023 with the IRS within twenty-seven months of its creation. This form is available online.

When the organization files Form 1023 within the prescribed time, the tax exemption is valid from the date of incorporation. If the nonprofit files Form 1023 after twenty-seven months of incorporation, the tax exemption is likely to start from the filing date forward.

Depending on the size of the organization, Form 1023-EZ, a streamlined version of the 1023 can be used and filed electronically. However, first the eligibility worksheet on the instructions for 1023-EZ must be filled out to be sure the organization meets all the requirements. The worksheet requests information on the size of the organization, assets, income, and types of activities. A sample 1023-EZ form follows.

Form **1023-EZ**	**Streamlined Application for Recognition of Exemption Under Section 501(c)(3) of the Internal Revenue Code**	OMB No. 1545-0056
(June 2014)	▸ **Do not enter social security numbers on this form as it may be made public.**	Note: *If exempt status is approved, this application will be open for public inspection.*
Department of the Treasury Internal Revenue Service	▸ Information about Form 1023-EZ and its separate instructions is at *www.irs.gov/form1023*.	

☐ Check this box to attest that you have completed the Form 1023-EZ Eligibility Worksheet in the current instructions, are eligible to apply for exemption using Form 1023-EZ, and have read and understand the requirements to be exempt under section 501(c)(3).

Part I   Identification of Applicant

1a Full Name of Organization

b Address (number, street, and room/suite). If a P.O. box, see instructions. | **c** City | **d** State | **e** Zip Code + 4

2 Employer Identification Number | **3** Month Tax Year Ends (MM) | **4** Person to Contact if More Information is Needed

5 Contact Telephone Number | **6** Fax Number (optional) | **7** User Fee Submitted

8 List the names, titles, and mailing addresses of your officers, directors, and/or trustees. (If you have more than five, see instructions.)

First Name:	Last Name:		Title:	
Street Address:	City:	State:	Zip Code + 4:	
First Name:	Last Name:		Title:	
Street Address:	City:	State:	Zip Code + 4:	
First Name:	Last Name:		Title:	
Street Address:	City:	State:	Zip Code + 4:	
First Name:	Last Name:		Title:	
Street Address:	City:	State:	Zip Code + 4:	
First Name:	Last Name:		Title:	
Street Address:	City:	State:	Zip Code + 4:	

9 a Organization's Website (if available):
b Organization's Email (optional):

Part II   Organizational Structure

1 To file this form, you must be a corporation, an unincorporated association, or a trust. **Check the box** for the type of organization.
☐ Corporation   ☐ Unincorporated association   ☐ Trust

2 ☐ **Check this box** to attest that you have the organizing document necessary for the organizational structure indicated above.
(See the instructions for an explanation of **necessary organizing documents**.)

3 Date incorporated if a corporation, or formed if other than a corporation (MMDDYYYY): _____

4 State of incorporation or other formation: _____

5 Section 501(c)(3) requires that your organizing document must limit your purposes to one or more exempt purposes within section 501(c)(3).
☐ **Check this box** to attest that your organizing document contains this limitation.

6 Section 501(c)(3) requires that your organizing document must not expressly empower you to engage, otherwise than as an insubstantial part of your activities, in activities that in themselves are not in furtherance of one or more exempt purposes.
☐ **Check this box** to attest that your organizing document does not expressly empower you to engage, otherwise than as an insubstantial part of your activities, in activities that in themselves are not in furtherance of one or more exempt purposes.

7 Section 501(c)(3) requires that your organizing document must provide that upon dissolution, your remaining assets be used exclusively for section 501(c)(3) exempt purposes. Depending on your entity type and the state in which you are formed, this requirement may be satisfied by operation of state law.
☐ **Check this box** to attest that your organizing document contains the dissolution provision required under section 501(c)(3) or that you do not need an express dissolution provision in your organizing document because you rely on the operation of state law in the state in which you are formed for your dissolution provision.

For Paperwork Reduction Act Notice, see the instructions.   Catalog No. 66267N   Form **1023-EZ** (6-2014)

Form 1023-EZ (6-2014)   Page **2**

Part III   Your Specific Activities

1 Enter the appropriate 3-character NTEE Code that best describes your activities (See the instructions): _____

2 To qualify for exemption as a section 501(c)(3) organization, you must be organized and operated exclusively to further one or more of the following purposes. By checking the box or boxes below, you attest that you are organized and operated exclusively to further the purposes indicated. **Check all that apply.**

☐ Charitable   ☐ Religious   ☐ Educational
☐ Scientific   ☐ Literary   ☐ Testing for public safety
☐ To foster national or international amateur sports competition   ☐ Prevention of cruelty to children or animals

3 To qualify for exemption as a section 501(c)(3) organization, you must:
- Refrain from supporting or opposing candidates in political campaigns in any way.
- Ensure that your net earnings do not inure in whole or in part to the benefit of private shareholders or individuals (that is, board members, officers, key management employees, or other insiders).
- Not further non-exempt purposes (such as purposes that benefit private interests) more than insubstantially.
- Not be organized or operated for the primary purpose of conducting a trade or business that is not related to your exempt purpose(s).
- Not devote more than an insubstantial part of your activities attempting to influence legislation or, if you make a section 501(h) election, not normally make expenditures in excess of expenditure limitations outlined in section 501(h).
- Not provide commercial-type insurance as a substantial part of your activities.

☐ **Check this box** to attest that you have not conducted and will not conduct activities that violate these prohibitions and restrictions.

4 Do you or will you attempt to influence legislation? . . . . ☐ Yes ☐ No
(If yes, consider filing Form 5768. See the instructions for more details.)

5 Do you or will you pay compensation to any of your officers, directors, or trustees? . . . . ☐ Yes ☐ No
(Refer to the instructions for a definition of **compensation**.)

6 Do you or will you donate funds to or pay expenses for individual(s)? . . . . ☐ Yes ☐ No

7 Do you or will you conduct activities or provide grants or other assistance to individual(s) or organization(s) outside the United States? . . . . ☐ Yes ☐ No

8 Do you or will you engage in financial transactions (for example, loans, payments, rents, etc.) with any of your officers, directors, or trustees, or any entities they own or control? . . . . ☐ Yes ☐ No

9 Do you or will you have unrelated business gross income of $1,000 or more during a tax year? . . . . . . ☐ Yes ☐ No

10 Do you or will you operate bingo or other gaming activities? . . . . ☐ Yes ☐ No

11 Do you or will you provide disaster relief? . . . . ☐ Yes ☐ No

Part IV   Foundation Classification

Part IV is designed to classify you as an organization that is either a private foundation or a public charity. Public charity status is a more favorable tax status than private foundation status.

1 If you qualify for public charity status, check the appropriate box (**1a – 1c** below) and skip to **Part V** below.

a ☐ **Check this box** to attest that you normally receive at least one-third of your support from public sources or you normally receive at least 10 percent of your support from public sources and you have other characteristics of a publicly supported organization. **Sections 509(a)(1) and 170(b)(1)(A)(vi).**

b ☐ **Check this box** to attest that you normally receive more than one-third of your support from a combination of gifts, grants, contributions, membership fees, and gross receipts (from permitted sources) from activities related to your exempt functions and normally receive not more than one-third of your support from investment income and unrelated business taxable income. **Section 509(a)(2).**

c ☐ **Check this box** to attest that you are operated for the benefit of a college or university that is owned or operated by a governmental unit. **Sections 509(a)(1) and 170(b)(1)(A)(iv).**

2 If you are not described in **1a** – **1c** above, you are a private foundation. As a private foundation, you are required by section 508(e) to have specific provisions in your organizing document, unless you rely on the operation of state law in the state in which you were formed to meet these requirements. These specific provisions require that you operate to avoid liability for private foundation excise taxes under sections 4941-4945.

☐ **Check this box** to attest that your organizing document contains the provisions required by section 508(e) or that your organizing document does not need to include the provisions required by section 508(e) because you rely on the operation of state law in your particular state to meet the requirements of section 508(e). (See the instructions for explanation of the section 508(e) requirements.)

Form **1023-EZ** (6-2014)

Form 1023-EZ (6-2014)   Page **3**

Part V   Reinstatement After Automatic Revocation

Complete this section only if you are applying for reinstatement of exemption after being automatically revoked for failure to file required annual returns or notices for three consecutive years, and you are applying for reinstatement under section 4 or 7 of Revenue Procedure 2014-11. (Check only one box.)

1   ☐ **Check this box** if you are seeking retroactive reinstatement under section 4 of Revenue Procedure 2014-11. By checking this box, you attest that you meet the specified requirements of section 4, that your failure to file was not intentional, and that you have put in place procedures to file required returns or notices in the future. (See the instructions for requirements.)

2   ☐ **Check this box** if you are seeking reinstatement under section 7 of Revenue Procedure 2014-11, effective the date you are filing this application.

Part VI   Signature

☐ I declare under the penalties of perjury that I am authorized to sign this application on behalf of the above organization and that I have examined this application, and to the best of my knowledge it is true, correct, and complete.

PLEASE SIGN HERE	(Type name of signer)	(Type title or authority of signer)
	(Signature of Officer, Director, Trustee, or other authorized official)	(Date)

Form **1023-EZ** (6-2014)

17

The fees payable with the Form 1023 vary with the size of the organization. In 2014, nonprofits with average annual gross receipts of over $10,000, pay $850 in fees. For smaller organizations, the fee is $400. Double check on the fee since it may change over the years. A nonprofit's staff should attach Form 8718 to the payment of the fee.

Churches do not typically need to file 1023—the IRS gives them tax exemption automatically. However, many choose to file the Form 1023 to affirm their status to donors and others.

Most organizations operate as tax-exempt and file nonprofit tax returns while waiting for the 1023 to be approved, which can be verified on the IRS website.

Determination Letter

The IRS "Determination" letter is the "holy grail" for a nonprofit, as it is the proof that a nonprofit is indeed tax-exempt and can receive tax-deductible donations. An organization should keep its Determination letter in a safe place, make copies of it, and keep them secure as well, because they will be very useful.

In the past, the IRS would issue an Advance Ruling letter before its Final Determination letter. Recently, the IRS streamlined this process for 501(c)(3) organizations, mailing a Determination letter upon approval of the nonprofit. There is no need to file Form 8734 anymore. If the Determination letter is lost, the IRS sends out "Affirmation" letters, confirming the tax-exempt status.

Note that the IRS may revoke 501(c)(3) tax-exempt status for various reasons, such as the failure to file tax returns for three consecutive years or excessive lobbying activities. Such organizations may promote legislation up to a certain point but cannot participate in political activity, including endorsing candidates for public office.

Sometimes the IRS makes mistakes and nonprofits lose their tax exemption, so be sure to look at the IRS Master List often. If you find problems that are not resolved promptly, try using the IRS Taxpayer Assistance Program.

Some businesses and foundations websites allow for online grant applications, which match the Employer Identification number with the IRS database automatically. If the number does not match, the organization cannot apply for assistance online. Therefore, it is important to ensure the information in the Master Database is correct and routinely updated.

Note that individual states, counties, and cities have different compliance requirements for nonprofits. For example, in California, organizations' founders must file Form 3500, "Submission of Exemption Request," after receiving the tax exemption from the IRS.

Next are sample IRS Determination and Affirmation letters.

Determination letter

INTERNAL REVENUE SERVICE
P. O. BOX 2508
CINCINNATI, OH 45201

DEPARTMENT OF THE TREASURY

Date: **MAR 30 2007**

Employer Identification Number:

DLN:

Contact Person:

T.U# .

Contact Telephone Number:

Accounting Period Ending:
June 30
Public Charity Status:
170(b)(1)(A)(vi)
Form 990 Required:
Yes
Effective Date of Exemption:
January 24, 2007
Contribution Deductibility:
Yes
Advance Ruling Ending Date:
June 30, 2011

Dear Applicant:

We are pleased to inform you that upon review of your application for tax exempt status we have determined that you are exempt from Federal income tax under section 501(c)(3) of the Internal Revenue Code. Contributions to you are deductible under section 170 of the Code. You are also qualified to receive tax deductible bequests, devises, transfers or gifts under section 2055, 2106 or 2522 of the Code. Because this letter could help resolve any questions regarding your exempt status, you should keep it in your permanent records.

Organizations exempt under section 501(c)(3) of the Code are further classified as either public charities or private foundations. During your advance ruling period, you will be treated as a public charity. Your advance ruling period begins with the effective date of your exemption and ends with advance ruling ending date shown in the heading of the letter.

Shortly before the end of your advance ruling period, we will send you Form 8734, Support Schedule for Advance Ruling Period. You will have 90 days after the end of your advance ruling period to return the completed form. We will then notify you, in writing, about your public charity status.

Please see enclosed Information for Exempt Organizations Under Section 501(c)(3) for some helpful information about your responsibilities as an exempt organization.

Letter 1045 (DO/CG)

-2-

Sincerely,

Enclosures: Information for Organizations Exempt Under Section 501(c)(3)
Statute Extension

Letter 1045 (DO/CG)

Affirmation letter

IRS Department of the Treasury
Internal Revenue Service
P.O. Box 2508
Cincinnati OH 45201

In reply refer to:
Sep. 27, 2010   LTR 4168C   ED

00015111
BODC: TE

Employer Identification Number:
Person to Contact:
Toll Free Telephone Number:

Dear Taxpayer:

This is in response to your Sep. 16, 2010, request for information regarding your tax-exempt status.

Our records indicate that you were recognized as exempt under section 501(c)(3) of the Internal Revenue Code in a determination letter issued in March 1995.

Our records also indicate that you are not a private foundation within the meaning of section 509(a) of the Code because you are described in section(s) 509(a)(1) and 170(b)(1)(A)(vi).

Donors may deduct contributions to you as provided in section 170 of the Code. Bequests, legacies, devises, transfers, or gifts to you or for your use are deductible for Federal estate and gift tax purposes if they meet the applicable provisions of sections 2055, 2106, and 2522 of the Code.

Please refer to our website www.irs.gov/eo for information regarding filing requirements. Specifically, section 6033(j) of the Code provides that failure to file an annual information return for three consecutive years results in revocation of tax-exempt status as of the filing due date of the third return for organizations required to file.

If you have any questions, please call us at the telephone number shown in the heading of this letter.

Sincerely yours,

<u>Summary</u>

Nonprofits are a growing sector of the U.S. economy that cannot be ignored as they provide important goods and services to many communities, such as shelter for the homeless. The nonprofits focused on in this publication are the ones identified as tax-exempt under 501(c)(3), such as charities and social services organizations. These organizations may receive government grants and use dedicated volunteers who must be properly managed.

The IRS is the federal entity that approves and maintains tax exemptions, although states may mandate their specific requirements as well. The IRS Determination and Affirmation letters are proof of an organization's tax-exempt status. Additionally, the IRS keeps a "Master Database" of tax-exempt organizations for public information at its website, www.irs.gov, which must be reviewed regularly.

3

Typical Structure of Nonprofits

"Men love to organize."

James Mooney, U.S. business executive (1884-1957)

Nonprofits and for-profit organizations can look the same on the surface. Both offer goods and services, may charge people, and provide classes, etc., but there is one main difference:

✓ **Nonprofits are not interested in making a profit.**

The nonprofit's goal is to provide a public service, not to enrich owners. Ownership does not even exist in the nonprofit world. Such organizations do not issue stocks or dividends; they are not part of the stock market. Their financial statements do not present "Owner's Equity" or "Stockholder Equity" sections. However, someone "minds the store." Many people—stakeholders—are often involved in the daily operation and success of the nonprofit.

Some typical stakeholders of a nonprofit organization are:

- Board of Directors
- Donors
- Grantors
- Banks
- Volunteers
- Community

Besides these "watchers," the nonprofit's founders often actively participate as members of the board of directors, helping with funding and program leadership. These passionate individuals have a lot of emotional attachment to the nonprofit, providing a vision for management and the community.

A vision is important, but the organization should also have a structure to ensure smooth operation and proper delivery of services. To this end, many nonprofits employ a president, vice-presidents, finance manager, etc., to supervise different sections. As with any business, size matters, and many large organizations are set up into "chapters" reporting to a headquarter office.

The board of directors and other jobs within a nonprofit can be filled by volunteers, including the role of president. Many nonprofits are run entirely by volunteers.

Each section of an organization must work together to fulfill the nonprofit's mission effectively and efficiently. Nonprofits must be well managed to survive the fiscal and other constraints of the sector, especially in tough economic times.

Furthermore, grantors often require certain minimum management standards, making it essential for nonprofits to implement controls and reliable reporting mechanisms to be viable. Many universities offer programs in nonprofit management and leadership, highlighting the specific needs of this sector.

Operational Areas

Any business needs a structure to operate effectively, and nonprofits are no different. Similar to for-profits, nonprofits try to operate with a method and within budget. Nonprofits must run efficient operations and demonstrate measurable outcomes because they are accountable to donors, board members, and the government.

As in any business sector, an effective framework must be present behind the scenes to keep things running smoothly. This is especially true in the nonprofit sector where operations support the organization in a number of functional sections, including:

- Office management
- Program management
- Accounting and finance
- Administration
- Human resources
- Information technology
- Marketing and development

These functions, reflecting operations, can be classified into three areas, all supervised by the board of directors:

- Programs/Services
- Management and General
- Fundraising

The "top boss" is the board of directors that oversee all areas. Many nonprofits retain executive directors who report to the board, while all departments report to him/her. Below is a typical organizational chart of a nonprofit:

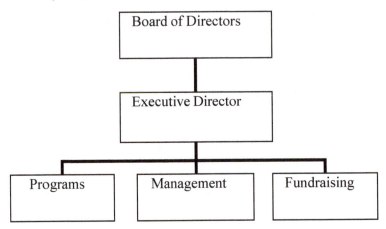

Identification of the three main areas of nonprofit operations (programs, management, and fundraising) is crucial to set up proper accounting systems, internal controls, reporting, and management.

If you plan to research nonprofits, www.Guidestar.org is a good resource. This comprehensive online database lists more than 1.8 million organizations, including their mission statements, fiscal information, and copies of tax returns. Users can access basic information free of charge.

Nonprofits' tax returns and financial statements are organized in three areas: programs, administration, and fundraising.

An issue for most nonprofits is how to manage a growing organization effectively. Many founders of nonprofits are not managers and do not possess a background in management. They may be "program" people who have created the nonprofit to fulfill personal goals, but management is often not their expertise. Sometimes the founders do not see the need for a formal organizational structure of the nonprofit, which may hurt the nonprofit's operations.

It is important for founders and boards of directors to realize this issue and to find proper personnel or volunteers to fill out the needed spots. I have seen small organizations fail to follow their mission statements because they did not possess a basic infrastructure, management, and personnel to deal with complex operation requirements

Programs

Without programs, nonprofits cannot exist; therefore, programs are the most important area of an organization. They must link to the organization's mission statement to be well-focused and effective.

✓ **The mission statement is so important that tax Form 990 specifically requests it.**

Significance

Programs are the heart of any nonprofit organization. If the purpose of an organization is to help the homeless, the nonprofit will offer programs in accordance with this goal. Such programs are likely to involve food distribution and mental health evaluation.

It can tricky to identify programs properly. Sometimes, a program in one place can be fundraising in another. For instance, an organization sells used clothes in a thrift shop. The thrift shop is most likely part of the fundraising area and not a program. However, if the organization provides job training for teens, then the thrift shop could be part of a program, especially if it has teens training in the shop's operations.

Managing Programs

Program management involves many issues, such as connecting to the mission statement and costs control.

Mission Statement- The clearer and simpler the mission statement, the easier it is to create major programs. Suppose a nonprofit's mission statement is to "provide temporary shelter to the homeless." It is simple and focused. If the organization hosts a car race as part of a program, for example, it will have troubles justifying how such a program is linked to the mission statement.

An organization with the mission statement "helping people to become self-sufficient" is too general, increasing the chances of confusion. The more focused the mission statement, the easier it is to develop well-directed programs.

"Mission creep" happens when certain stakeholders want to take the nonprofit in directions not really related to its mission statement. Donors and grantors may also cause this problem by offering funds for programs outside the scope of the organization's mission.

Program Expense Allocation- Another concern of nonprofits within the program section is its expenses. This is pertinent for nonprofits financial statements and grant accounting. According to the Jewish proverb, *"If charity cost nothing, the world would be full of philanthropists."* Programs do not run for free. Their costs are usually identified as:

- Direct
- Indirect

Direct costs or expenses can be easily assigned to a program, such as art supplies for an art program. The nonprofit knows for sure how much it spends on supplies for this program. There is no doubt. Direct costs are usually supported by bills and time sheets showing clearly that the expense belongs to a certain program.

Indirect costs or expenses, also known as overhead, are those affecting more than one program. They cannot be clearly identified as belonging to one program or another. For example, costs of fire insurance on a building that houses all programs and operations may be considered an indirect cost. Nonprofits assign such indirect costs to each program according to a reasonable basis, a process known as a "cost allocation."

Expense/ cost allocations to programs and other sections can be a challenge to calculate. Donors, especially government grantors, are interested in cost allocations to make sure they are not paying for personal expenses and other non-authorized uses of the money. Identifying direct costs is relatively easy, but nonprofits may have problems dealing with allocations because they can be complex, using different bases for each cost.

Indirect costs may be outside the program section, such as accounting department costs, or they could be part of the programs, such as a postage machine used by many programs. Since the definition of indirect costs may vary from one organization to another, it is best to have written policies regarding this issue. The federal government has its own definition about indirect costs, calculations, and application of indirect cost rates, which are important when nonprofits receive federal grants.

When reviewing indirect cost reimbursements, nonprofits must keep good records, including backup calculations and the basis for the indirect cost allocation to a program. If not, grantors may not reimburse or fund certain costs, which can spell disaster.

✓ **Accounting systems should identify and report on program expenses—both direct and indirect.**

The chart of accounts identifies direct and indirect costs, keeping program expenses separate from other sections. Nonprofits must also segregate revenues and expenses by individual programs. For example, nonprofits should separate supply expenses from Program A from supply expenses from Program B. The chart of accounts of nonprofits often has long segments to accommodate the need to separate the expenses at the program and grant levels.

Many organizations do the allocations for indirect costs on a spreadsheet, using labor costs, square footage, or another basis that makes sense. Indirect costs can be assigned to "pools" first and then the pools are allocated to each program.

Not surprisingly, the program section is expected to report the most expenses in financial statements. Since programs are the reason for the organization's existence, donors and grantors carefully review this area as compared with the others. Was program cost 80 percent of total costs? 25 percent? The higher the percentage, the better off the organization is in the eyes of donors.

Program Challenge

Measuring Success- Measuring a program's success is a challenge for many organizations. Donors (and grantors) want to know if programs are working, and if they should continue funding. Measuring the impact of a social program in a community can be tricky to evaluate and measure, for instance.

Attendance can be a sign of success in some programs, but this may not always be the case. For example, a nonprofit may implement a hotline program, where the number of calls received is a good measuring stick. However, if the hotline's goal is to provide babysitting referrals, the number of kids placed, rather than the number of calls, would be more indicative of success.

As programs are set up, nonprofits must be aware of the question, "How can we prove the program works?" The organization may create a baseline to compare "before" and "after." Programs should focus on measurable goals, such as to serve 200 families, or to provide food for 100 homeless people. If a program has the goal of improving the mental health of 100 men, then there must be a way to measure not only the number of men, but also the improvements within these men. These measurements can be observations and notes by clinicians or results of tests given to program participants.

To measure success properly, people involved in delivering programs must understand the concepts and be trained in methods of gathering the required information. Otherwise, the documentation may be sloppy, and the organization could lose a lot of money.

Management and General

Per Peter Drucker, *"Management is doing things right; leadership is doing the right things."* Management is the backbone of any nonprofit. It provides a structure for the programs and fundraising sections to work effectively.

Significance

The "management and general" area is composed of all tasks not directly related to programs or to fundraising. Nonprofits may call this "Administration," "General and Administration," or "G&A." Typically, the management and general section comprises:

- Planning and strategy—both long and short-term
- Accounting/finance activities, including budget preparation and financial reporting
- Human resources processes—hiring and keeping the right people, employee benefits
- Risk management—insurance issues, safety
- Legal issues—dealing with lawsuits and other legal matters

- Construction oversight and management
- Building maintenance
- IT—computer and software purchases and maintenance
- Safety of assets
- Investment decisions

✓ **The G&A area typically reports the second highest expense on financial statements, after programs.**

Managing G&A

Decisions made by G&A affect all functions of a nonprofit, so they must be made carefully. An organization cannot fulfill its mission if it does not have proper insurance, or if bills are not paid. Providing an extra layer of protection, the board of directors, whose costs are usually classified as G&A, may review large expenses, including major construction costs.

An interesting duty of management is to assess in-kind donations—gifts of things—before they are accepted. A donation of land or a building seems great at first; however, upon further scrutiny, it may hold the organization responsible for cleaning up hazardous materials, etc. Typically, G&A managers decide to accept only large donations that make sense to the organization. For instance, a nonprofit may not accept a work of art because it cannot afford the extra insurance. Development staff may determine if the in-kind donation is acceptable, but most often I have seen G&A personnel performing this function.

G&A may be a combination of direct and indirect costs, although it is normally considered an "indirect cost" or "overhead."

One of the issues I noticed about G&A is related to committee-based decisions. Instead of one person deciding, the nonprofit forms a committee to perform this task. This method may not be the best for the nonprofit. For example, an organization tried to implement a new nationwide system for donations. Nobody at the executive level had the experience or the knowledge to make decisions about it. A committee, comprised of employees at different levels, formed to make major decisions regarding the new system. Up to a certain point, committee decisions were valid and made sense. However, the organization really needed a chief information officer to oversee this process and to make sound decisions in this situation. This employee was hired after the committee made numerous bad and costly decisions.

It is better to appoint one qualified person to make decisions regarding issues he/she has experience with, rather than to gather an unqualified group of people to make decisions that often are not beneficial to the nonprofit.

Administrative Challenges

A challenge to G&A is securing funding to cover its costs. Donors, especially foundations and wealthy individuals, may refuse to donate for G&A, preferring their money to go to a specific cause or research. Their reluctance in allocating funds for G&A is likely due to the fear of abuse by executives, partly because of many scandalous stories in the media regarding these cases.

Psychologically, it is more heartwarming to donate to a specific program, rather than to general operations of an organization. The result is that organizations are required to use other funds to cover G&A expenses. Many times galas and other fundraising efforts are used to cover G&A/overhead. This problem has reached a crisis point in many nonprofits, where funds are restricted for programs only, and nothing can be spent on management. As we know, without management, the nonprofit cannot properly fulfill its mission and programs; therefore, the organization may close if it only has program-restricted funds.

Due to funding cuts, some organizations' G&A managers may decide to "borrow" funds from restricted programs to cover other areas, including administration. Nonprofits should avoid this situation because not only does it show bad cash management, it may also be prohibited by grant stipulations and state laws.

Currently, to resolve this issue, many nonprofits require donors to allocate a portion of grants to G&A and overhead, or they will not accept the money.

Fundraising

Nonprofits often call the fundraising function as "Development." The closest counterpart in the for-profit world would be "Marketing." While for-profit marketing's goal is to increase sales, development's goal is to increase donations, grants, and other revenues.

Significance

Fundraising/Development departments market the organization, search for funding sources, and monitor amounts received. Fundraisers plan and work on fundraising activities, such as golf tournaments, dinner parties, and telethons. They may also write grant proposals for foundations, businesses, and governments. In addition, development people may set up seminars regarding the virtues of gifting and adding donations to estate planning.

Normally, a nonprofit is not in the business of fundraising. Although this should not be an organization's most important goal, nonprofits do need to survive and maintain programs. Fundraisers are used to maintain current funding and find other sources of aid, including business grants. This is true, even if nonprofits are funded mostly with government grants. Often, the money from government is not enough to cover for all overhead and other "extra" costs.

Managing Fundraising

The fundraising department's goal is to make the organization's programs attractive to donors, who may be individuals, foundations, businesses, governments, or other nonprofits. Often, fundraising is about selling a new program, improving or changing existing ones. The idea is for donors to be matched with nonprofits' needs and programs. Who would be interested in donating to a certain cause? Maybe the organization needs to obtain more funds to help the increasing homeless population—who would be interested in this program?

The development department creates brochures and marketing materials to sell the organization to prospective donors and grantors. They can make presentations, set up radio and TV spots, etc. Larger nonprofits may retain a director or vice-president of development and build an entire department dedicated to raising funds. In other organizations, this function is outsourced and used on an "as needed" basis. In addition, many times, board members are the best fundraisers for the organization.

✓ **Nonprofits must be flexible and have the ability to accept credit card and online donations.**

Fundraising departments may also work with donors' employers that may match donations of employees, increasing the overall funding for the organization. If an employee gives $10, the employer may match with $5, $10, or even $20.

Donors should feel welcome by everyone in an organization, not just by development personnel. Many times donors call the accounting department or other departments to make donations over the phone, and they should feel comfortable doing so.

Fundraising Challenges

Bad Economy- As expected, when the economy is weak, it is hard to obtain donations. Fundraisers may offer donors the option of making donations in installments to facilitate the process. They may also setup sweepstakes to attract more gifts.

Costs of Fundraising- Fundraising managers should be creative in decreasing the costs of campaigns and events. For example, nonprofits should take advantage of the special postal rates for tax-exempt organizations and negotiate deals with venues for events. Many places offer discounts for nonprofits. Fundraisers should know about the sale/use-tax laws in the states where they may be exempt from paying or collecting taxes on certain transactions.

Additionally, fundraisers must consider all costs, including overhead, when evaluating fundraising activities. When an event is held at a separate venue, rent and other costs are considered, but when events are held in-house, the cost of building maintenance and other not-so-obvious costs are often ignored.

Confusing Strategy- One of the problems noted with fundraising is regarding organizations raising funds for one cause and then placing the funds into a general fund and using them for operations, rather than for the program originally shown. This situation is neither ethical nor fair to donors and places the organization in a potential liability situation because donors may complain that they donated under false pretenses. Funds specified for a cause must be separated in the accounting books and not be mixed with other money. To avoid confusion, some nonprofits deposit restricted money in a separate bank account.

Compensation- Another challenge to the fundraising area is compensation. Fundraisers may get bonuses for campaigns, but paying them a percentage of the money raised is not advised, according to the Association of Fundraising Professionals (www.afpnet.org).

We have all heard of fundraising firms that end up keeping most of the money. They may offer to fundraise "for cheap," but end up with most of the funds. So, organizations should apply due diligence when dealing with fundraising firms. Nonprofits should also avoid hiring firms belonging to board members or other related parties to avoid problems with private inurement, where one or more persons take advantage of the organization for personal gain.

✓ **Many donors do not like "over-solicitations" and can become testy. Be careful.**

Sheila Shanker

<u>Summary</u>

Nonprofits' operations can be classified as Programs, Administration (G&A), and Fundraising. These three sections work in concert for the organization to follow its mission. Programs, the heart of the organization, involve direct and indirect costs, and measuring success is one of the issues with this area.

G&A is the backbone of operations, including accounting and HR functions. A challenge here is to obtain funds to cover its expenses. Many donors want to fund programs but not G&A.

Fundraising is the marketing and development of an organization. This area handles special events, donors, and grant proposals. One of its challenges is to obtain funds during a bad economy.

4

Accounting Basics

"Money is better than poverty, if only for financial reasons."

Woody Allen

Nonprofits, like any other business, need money to survive. Good deeds can carry an organization only so far, and with the money comes the accounting practices, which are a bit different from the for-profit world. Since nonprofits are not in the business of making a profit, accounting differences between for-profits and nonprofits warrant some discussion.

A good approach is to assume that accounting for nonprofit organizations is the same as for-profits, but with an extra level of detail. It is similar to project accounting. Not all revenues are equal, and they are not recognized in the same way. Since revenue may relate to a specific program or grant, nonprofits need to track the source and kind of revenue carefully. On the same track, an expense is not just an expense, as it could be related to a specific program or grant and cannot be mixed with other expenses in the accounting books. Nonprofits must track revenues and expenses in such a detailed manner that it may surprise people accustomed to the for-profit model.

GAAP

GAAP stands for "Generally Accepted Accounting Principles." These are guidelines, usually promulgated by FASB as part of the Accounting Standards Codification (ASC), to guide accounting and fiscal reporting in the U.S. ASC Document 958 contains guidelines for nonprofit accounting and financial statements.

Accounting for nonprofits is also known as "fund accounting." The word "fund" means different things to various people. For our purposes in this publication, funds and net assets refer to the same thing.

The main purpose of fund accounting (nonprofit accounting) is the stewardship of economic resource, ensuring they are spent in compliance with legal or other requirements. Rather than being concerned with investors' interests, fund accounting focuses on maintaining adequate funds (net assets) to provide for present and future programs and services.

Cash or Accrual

Nonprofits have the choice of using the cash or accrual methods in accounting, although the accrual method is the one recognized by GAAP. Under the cash basis, revenue and expenses are recognized when money exchanges hands. Therefore, when a nonprofit receives a bill, it does not recognize it as an expense until it is paid. On the other hand, under the accrual basis, the bill may be recognized as an expense even if it is not paid. According to the accrual method, revenues and expenses are recognized as they happen, rather than when money is received or paid.

Cash Basis

The main advantage of the cash basis of accounting is that it reflects the current cash situation. It is simple. Revenues shown are revenues received, while expenses presented are those paid. Many times board members and management prefer cash basis financial statement because they can understand them better.

Additionally, cash basis accounting is conservative in recognizing revenues. If large pledges are not collectible, the cash method may provide a more realistic view of the financial situation of the organization because it only reports on money received (and paid).

However, cash basis accounting has inherent weaknesses, such as not recognizing future revenues or expenses. This makes planning difficult. For instance, if the organization is supposed to pay $100,000 within the next few months, it is better to show this liability now and not be surprised later on.

Another weakness of the cash basis is that the time of revenue recognition is not the same as expense recognition. The timing is off and may create confusion; such as when a nonprofit pays an expense of $100,000, but has not received the revenue yet. At first glance, this will show the organization with a loss, but in reality, the revenue will be shown later under the cash basis of accounting.

Cash basis would not be appropriate if a nonprofit estimates the cost of a program now and most of bills are received and paid in the future. Expenses may be "forgotten," especially if they show up months later. Consequently, reporting the programs on the cash basis may contain incomplete information.

When there are no major receivables or payables, differences between the cash and accrual basis may not be material. In addition, organizations may be on a cash basis and then adjustments can be made for reporting purposes without major consequences.

Accrual Basis

There are many good reasons for a nonprofit to report on an accrual basis, rather than on a cash basis. Not only is the accrual method accepted by GAAP, it is also endorsed by the IFRS—International Financial Reporting Standards in accordance with standards and interpretations adopted by the International Accounting Standards Board (IASB). These international standards guide many companies worldwide, including the U.S., which is in the process of adopting them. The IFRS may not have much effect now on U.S. nonprofits, but it is just a matter of time before its requirements will start trickling down to the nonprofit sector.

An advantage of the accrual method is the matching of revenues to expenses, giving users a better view of the economic condition of an organization. When an event occurs, for instance, revenues and expenses for the event are shown together by using accounts payable, receivable, deferred revenues and other items not employed in the cash basis of accounting.

Another benefit of accrual accounting is that it includes many useful reports. For example, if an organization shows $300,000 in revenue and uses the accrual basis, information on aging of receivables would be useful to determine the details of amounts still owed to the nonprofit.

However, the accrual basis, with its technical concepts such as deferred revenue, can be complicated for non-accountants to understand. Usually, when presenting an accrual report to managers who are not knowledgeable about accounting, I explain how much of the revenues showing up are still owed and how much of the expenses have been really paid. Next is an example of a report using cash versus accrual methods—The Statement of Financial Position, the nonprofit's version of a balance sheet:

The Do-Good Organization
Statement of Financial Position
December 31, 20X1

		Cash Basis	Accrual Basis
Assets			
	Cash	10,000	10,000
	Interest receivable	0	3,000
	Pledges receivable	0	5,000
Total Assets:		10,000	18,000
Liabilities			
	Accrued expenses	0	7,000
Unrestricted Net Assets		10,000	11,000
Total Liabilities and Net Assets:		10,000	18,000

This report shows accrued (unpaid) expense of $7,000 that is significant to the organization. This organization would benefit from the accrual basis of accounting. If managers only review the cash numbers, they will be misled and will not be aware of the accrued expenses – expenses that will be paid in the future, but they happened in 20X1.This could be utilities that belong in one period, but are paid in the future, after the services are provided.

In spite of the disadvantages of the cash basis of accounting, the reality is that many small nonprofits use cash or modified cash basis where some transactions are recognized using cash while others are not. At year-end, the accounting books are adjusted for accrual items. This is usually an acceptable practice done by many nonprofits, especially smaller ones.

Net Assets

Nonprofits' financial statements utilize a different vocabulary than for-profits'. Terms like "Net Assets" may puzzle some readers. Net asset, also known as a fund, is a basic entity for a nonprofit organization. While in the for-profit world, "Retained Earnings" is presented, in the nonprofit sector net assets are shown.

A net asset is like a "bucket." Nonprofits place each revenue and expense in a specific bucket. For instance, if a nonprofit has $100 in postage expenses, the question is not only which account this expense should be booked to, but also which net asset (bucket) the expense belongs to. If there are departments, then the expense needs to be booked in the right account, department, and net asset. Because of the details required, nonprofit organizations' accounts may have many digits.

Some organizations meet this challenge by creating many restricted sub-funds, one for each purpose. Others keep historical spreadsheets on what each fund or sub-fund contains. Many do both because it is too easy to "forget" money received. Be aware of this common problem—a typical issue for many nonprofits.

Because of the detail level required in fund accounting, a "roll-forward schedule" is a common annual report provided. The schedule shows the beginning balances of all net assets and transactions, as well as the ending balances. Next is an example of this type of schedule:

Roll Forward - Restricted Funds Worksheet		Year 20XX			
Segment #		Beg. Balance	Increases	Decreases	End. Balance
503	Scholarship	100,000	40,000	(15,000)	125,000
504	Book Fund	50,000	3,000	(1,000)	52,000
509	Building Fund	125,000	-	(30,000)	95,000
	Total Restricted	275,000	43,000	(46,000)	272,000

Some nonprofits keep separate checking accounts for each net asset and reconcile the balance on each net asset with the books at least once a year. The point is to remember all monies and to spend them appropriately.

Net Asset Types

Net assets provide a structure for the organization to identify and track different types of revenues and expenses related to each of them. They organize the accounting data, so that queries and reporting can be done easily.

In addition, nonprofits use net assets to segregate resources restricted by donors, law, or government. SFAS 117, used to be the official guidance on this topic. Now, FASB Accounting Standards Codification (ASC) provides the rules for nonprofits. Consequently, you may see references to both SFAS and ASC when researching nonprofit fiscal issues. The idea is to identify, classify and report on funds and not "bunch" them all together.

✓ **Net assets/ funds are not "assets."**

Nonprofits may consider net assets as projects with their own financial statements. Net assets, also known as assets less liabilities, are mechanisms to keep the fiscal information straight over the long term. To this end, a nonprofit may have more than one type of net asset to handle its operations. The three basic types of net assets are:

- o Unrestricted Net Assets

- o Temporarily Restricted Net Assets

- o Permanently Restricted Net Assets

Each of these net assets keeps information on certain revenues and expenses that are presented separately in the financial statements of nonprofits. See next an excerpt of the Statement of Activities, the Income Statement of nonprofits.

The Helping Organization
Statement of Activities
Year ended December 31, 20xx

		Unrest. Net Assets	Temp. Restricted Net Assets	Perm. Restricted Net Assets	Total
Revenue					
	Contributions	100,000	50,000	20,000	170,000
	Fees for service	55,000			55,000
	~	~	~	~	~
	~	~	~	~	~
	~	~	~	~	~
Ending Net Asset Balance		250,000	50,000	20,000	320,000

The example shows the Helping Organization receiving $100,000 in contributions, booked in the unrestricted net asset to be used in daily activities. Revenue of $50,000 showing under the temporarily restricted column was to be used in the future or for a specific program. The organization also received $20,000 classified under the permanently restricted net asset; most likely, it is an endowment to be held long term, while the nonprofit can spend income, such as interest.

Unrestricted Net Assets

Nonprofits utilize this net asset to run operations, day-to-day activities, and general transactions of the organization. Nonprofits may refer to this net asset as "General," "Unrestricted," "Current Unrestricted Fund," or "Operating Net Asset." This net asset/fund contains resources that are not restricted. All general donations are booked in this net asset. If an organization has no restrictions on donations, then these would show under the unrestricted net asset. As an example, suppose a nonprofit receives $10,000 to fund current activities. The amount is booked as revenue in the unrestricted fund.

Donations for a specific activity not part of general operations, such as a new food program for the homeless, are not booked into this net asset. Rather, these types of revenues are recognized as parts of another net asset.

✓ **Most expenses run through the unrestricted net asset, even though revenues may be booked in another net asset, such as temporarily restricted.**

An interesting sub-set of the unrestricted net asset is the "Board Designated Fund." Boards can designate funds to pay for certain projects. An example would be a "generosity fund" set up by the board for specific programs. The board could also change its mind and use the funds for something else. This is why this type of fund is part of the unrestricted net asset "umbrella" and not restricted. Only donors can restrict funds, not boards.

Unrestricted funds are important if the nonprofit has a debt covenant, such as loans or bonds. Many banks require a minimum balance in the unrestricted fund as part of the loan or bond deal.

Temporarily Restricted Net Assets

Nonprofits may call this net asset a "Restricted Net Asset," "Restricted Fund," or "Temporarily Restricted Fund." Organizations use this net asset for a specific purpose, as per the donors' wishes, which cannot be overridden by the board of directors. If a donor wants the money to go for brain cancer research only, board members cannot override this wish and apply the funds toward publications, for instance. As expected, donor approval is required for any changes.

To comply with donors' desires, organizations should exercise due diligence, including maintaining written documentation to justify the restrictions. If a donor does not want to put anything in writing, the organization could send a "thank you" note confirming the situation.

Donors can restrict funds for a specific activity, program, event, etc. However, there are limits. Many nonprofits implement policies about this issue to avoid confusion. Suppose a donor gives $100 to a program that does not exist. Should the organization return the funds to the donor? Should the organization recognize the donation in another similar program? Nonprofits' policies and procedures should cover these topics in detail to avoid confusion.

Organizations may create various temporarily restricted funds, such as for "scholarships," and any donations for scholarships are booked there. Funds set up should be functional enough to accommodate most of the restricted funds. However, when a nonprofit has too many restricted funds, management of such funds can become costly and cumbersome. Some common sense is valuable here.

✓ **Do not forget to look at the restricted net assets for budgeting— revenues classified there may cover significant costs.**

A major restricted activity may involve several stages like the situation of a capital campaign for construction. Some donors want to donate after construction has started, while others would like to donate for a specific room or classroom. In this case, separate sub-accounts within the temporary fund capital campaign "umbrella" could be set up.

Many times the donation is for the future, and the restriction is about time and/or actual expenses. Once the restriction is lifted, revenue is "released." As an example, suppose a donor gives $10,000 to defray expenses of a travel program for a school. The $10,000 is booked in the restricted fund. As travel expenses occur, revenue is released from temporarily restricted to the unrestricted net asset, "refunding" the unrestricted fund for the costs. Next is a summary of the transactions assuming the expenses happened $5,000 at a time.

	Unrestricted Net Asset	Temp. Restricted Net Asset
Donation to restricted net asset		10,000 increase revenue
Travel Expenses 1	5,000 increase expense	
Release from restriction	5,000 increase revenue	5,000 decrease revenue
Travel Expenses 2	5,000 increase expense	
Release from restriction	5,000 increase revenue	5,000 decrease revenue
Net Asset Balance	No effect	0 balance

Once the organization incurs $10,000 in travel expenses, the balance in the restricted fund would be zero. The total effect on the unrestricted fund will be zero because expenses were covered by restricted money.

An example of a timing restriction is a donation that can be used in the future because of a special anniversary. In this case, expenses do not matter. For example, a donor gives $5,000 to commemorate a tenth anniversary. On the day of the anniversary, the amount is released regardless of expenses incurred. A release based on a special date is "new" unrestricted money the organization can use as it sees fit. In contrast, a release to reimburse expenses is not "new"—the money has been spent.

Nonprofits can release net assets up to the balance in the restricted funds. If a restricted fund has a net asset balance of $20,000, then the organization can release up to $20,000 only. If a nonprofit does not have any restricted net assets, there is no need to release anything.

✓ **Balances on restricted net assets cannot be negative.**

Overall, restricted fund balances should decrease as expenses are booked, and net assets should be released as time progresses or expenses occur, depending on the restriction. The idea is for all temporarily restricted funds to zero out over time. If a net asset balance is negative, it is a sign of error since nonprofits cannot release/decrease revenues they do not have.

Permanently Restricted Net Assets

Many people leave money to charity in their names or their family's names as long-term gifts or endowments, often as part of estate planning. The idea is for the donation's principal to remain intact, while the nonprofit spends any income, such as dividends. Nonprofits recognize this donation type in the permanently restricted net asset, also known as an "endowment fund."

This net asset is often large and held in perpetuity, or for a very long time. Written documentation specifying the details of the donation is important. Information on any restrictions, applications of gains/losses and income is crucial, especially when the endowments lose value, such as during a recession.

Permanent net assets must be managed carefully to allow for enough operating funds. During challenging economic times, quite a few organizations were endowment-rich, but could not use the fund for day-to-day activities.

Traditionally, the larger the endowment fund, the stronger the organization's economic situation. Colleges are known for their large endowments. Harvard University had an endowment of about $31 billion in 2013.

To deal with the legalities of endowments, many states adopted the UPMIFA (Uniform Prudent Management of Institutional Funds Act), providing uniform rules related to endowment investments and expenses. Nonprofits should check with the states where they operate for specific laws regarding endowments. Some states allow for an inflation/deflation effect on investments, while others do not.

It is important to keep all documentation on permanently restricted funds safe. Sometimes the income from such funds is for specific programs or it could be used for administration. Since nonprofits keep the money in this net asset for a very long time, the documentation must be protected and available for the long-term. A summary of net assets follows:

Unrestricted	Shows most expenses	Balance increases with "releases"
Temporarily restricted	Shows no expenses with a few exceptions	Balance decreases with "releases"
Permanently restricted	Principal cannot be used	UPMIFA applies

Inter-fund Accounts

Inter-fund accounts link all funds or net assets. These accounts carry standard names to identify them easily, such as "Due to" and "Due from." They are similar to the inter-departmental or inter-company accounts in the for-profit world. These accounts are used to keep track of loans and any transactions between the funds. As their for-profit counterparts, they are internal entries that total up to zero at consolidated level.

Suppose a nonprofit has more than one unrestricted net asset, such as a general and board-designated fund. If the general fund borrows money from the designated one, "Due to/Due from accounts" are used to document the transaction. These accounts help to keep all net assets straight. Additionally, many nonprofits zero out these accounts before year-end to avoid confusion.

Net Assets Released from Restrictions Accounts

These inter-fund accounts are typical of the nonprofit sector with some similarity to the deferred revenue account (liability) used in the for-profit business. However, in the nonprofit world, a donation received that cannot be used right away (restricted) is recognized as part of the restricted net asset, not as deferred revenue.

When the restriction is met, the "Net Assets Released from Restrictions" accounts, also known as "release accounts," are used to decrease the restricted net asset and increase the unrestricted net asset. This is a bit similar to decreasing the deferred revenue and increasing the regular revenues in the for-profit world.

The "release" is presented in the Statement of Activities (Income Statement of nonprofits) as a positive number under the unrestricted net asset column and as a negative number under the temporarily restricted net asset column. Both positive and negative numbers should be the same.

Nonprofits should do these releasing entries often to keep the net asset balance numbers correct. Otherwise, the unrestricted net asset is likely to be understated and the temporarily restricted one could be overstated.

The journal entry to release funds is to debit the temporarily restricted fund and credit the unrestricted one. Below is an example of a release entry of $300.

Release of net assets- Restricted	300	
Release of net assets- Unrestricted		300

After the entry is booked, the temporarily restricted net assets are decreased, while the unrestricted net assets are increased by $300.

✓ **Release accounts are used for donations only, not exchanges, where a donor receives something in return for the money.**

Next is an example of a Statement of Activities, the summarized nonprofit "Income Statement" showing the release as part of revenues:

Do-good Organization
Statement of Activities
As of December 31, 20XX

	Unrestricted	Temporarily Restricted	Permanently Restricted	Total
Changes to Unrestricted Net Assets:				
Revenues and Gains:				
Public Contributions (net)	500,000		46,000	546,000
Investment Income	30,000			30,000
Net Assets Released from Restrictions	100,000	(100,000)	-	-
Total Revenues, Gains and other Support:	630,000	(100,000)	46,000	576,000
Total Expenses and Losses:				
Program Services	345,000			345,000
General Administration	125,000			125,000
Fund Raising	20,000			20,000
Total Expenses and Losses:	490,000			490,000
Increase in Net Assets	140,000	(100,000)	46,000	86,000
Net Assets at Beginning of Year	200,000	300,000	500,000	1,000,000
Net Assets at End of Year	340,000	200,000	546,000	1,086,000

Note in the example that the nonprofit released $100,000 from restriction. The numbers show up as positive under the unrestricted fund and as a negative under the temporarily restricted fund. The result in the total column is zero. This is always the case—the total across on the net assets released from restrictions should be zero. Some organizations present detailed release information, such as "Expiration of time restriction- United Way," so the release section may be more than one line, but it should always zero out across.

Nonprofits use release accounts because specific expenses happened, or a certain date arrived. Next are examples of entries illustrating both situations.

Example of release entry to cover expenses- Organization bought $500 worth of literacy books. Donations for literacy books have been kept in a restricted net asset. Cash for the expense came out of the general fund checking account. Relevant journal entries would be:

JE-1	GF- Book Expense	500	
	GF- Cash		500
	To buy book covered by restricted fund		

JE-2	RF- Net assets released from restrictions	500	
	GF- Net assets released from restrictions		500
	To release revenue restricted		

GF- General Fund- Unrestricted net assets

RF- Temporarily Restricted Fund/net assets

Next is an excerpt of a Statement of Activities (Income Statement of nonprofits) after these transactions occurred:

				Unrestricted	Temporarily Restricted
Revenues					
	Contributions				
	Other income				
	Net assets released from restriction			500	(500)
Total Revenues				500	(500)
Expenses					
	Program - Literacy Books			500	
	Management and General				
	Fund Raising				
Total Expenses				500	-
Change in net assets				0	(500)

Note that the end result with the unrestricted net asset is zero while the transactions decreased the temporarily restricted net asset by $500. As expected, this statement shows no expenses for temporarily restricted net asset, only for unrestricted. (If the nonprofit were to keep the restricted funds in separate bank accounts, then the restricted net asset would owe unrestricted $500.)

Example of release entries for timing- The organization received $10,000 for use only after Mary's birthday, which is today. The nonprofit has had this amount on the books since 2001, but it could not use it until today. The journal entry today will be:

RF-Net assets released from restriction   10,000

        GF-Net assets released from restriction   10,000

To release funds originally restricted by date.

GF- General Fund
RF- Restricted Fund

When net assets are released because of time, the money may be available for any expense. Nonprofits can use it for any purpose. The end result is that the unrestricted net asset increases because no expenses are associated with this donation. Next is an excerpt of a Statement of Activities after this journal entry:

			Unrestricted	Temporarily Restricted
Revenues				
	Contributions			
	Other income			
	Net assets released from restriction		10,000	(10,000)
Total Revenues			10,000	(10,000)
Expenses				
	Program - Literacy Books			
	Management and General			
	Fund Raising			
Total Expenses			0	-
Change in net assets			10,000	(10,000)

Some organizations keep releases from restriction in a separate spreadsheet with details, while others prefer to add to the description of the account or transaction. Clearly, documentation on the restrictions and releases is essential.

Since this official presentation can be confusing, many board members prefer to see details of the expenses as part of each fund, instead of a one-line item. Therefore, many organizations recognize the expenses on each temporarily restricted fund and at year-end, nonprofits adjust the numbers to comply with GAAP. Next are examples of an organization's financial statements before and after adjustments.

Before:

Internal Report of ABC Nonprofit
December 31, 20XX

	Unrestricted	Temporarily Restricted	Permanently Restricted	Total
Changes to Unrestricted Net Assets:				
Revenues and Gains:				
Public Contributions (net)	430,000		50,000	480,000
Investment Income	14,780			14,780
Net Assets Released from Restrictions	-		-	-
Total Revenues, Gains and other Support:	444,780	-	50,000	494,780
Total Expenses and Losses:				
Programs				-
Books		5,490		5,490
Scholarships		10,000		10,000
General Administration	125,000	-		125,000
Fundraising	20,000	-		20,000
Total Expenses and Losses:	145,000	15,490		160,490
Increase/Decrease in Net Assets	299,780	(15,490)	50,000	334,290
Net Assets at Beginning of Year	100,000	150,000	500,000	750,000
Net Assets at End of Year	399,780	134,510	550,000	1,084,290

This report shows expenses of $15,490 charged to each net asset for books and scholarships. Note that there was $150,000 as the beginning balance in the temporarily restricted net assets, so charging the expense amounts to this net asset type seems to be appropriate, although not presented according to official guidelines.

Next is the same report using GAAP rules. The idea is still the same, but the release is presented with revenues:

ABC Nonprofit
Statement of Activities
December 31, 20XX

	Unrestricted	Temporarily Restricted	Permanently Restricted	Total
Changes to Unrestricted Net Assets:				
Revenues and Gains:				
Public Contributions (net)	430,000		50,000	480,000
Investment Income	14,780			14,780
Net Assets Released from Restrictions	15,490	(15,490)	-	-
Total Revenues, Gains and other Support:	460,270	(15,490)	50,000	494,780
Total Expenses and Losses:				
Programs				
Books	5,490			5,490
Scholarships	10,000			10,000
General Administration	125,000	-		125,000
Fundraising	20,000	-		20,000
Total Expenses and Losses:	160,490	-		160,490
Increase/Decrease in Net Assets	299,780	(15,490)	50,000	334,290
Net Assets at Beginning of Year	100,000	150,000	500,000	750,000
Net Assets at End of Year	399,780	134,510	550,000	1,084,290

Overall, the ending balances in each fund did not change. For instance, the temporarily restricted net asset shows the balance of $134,510, regardless of which method is used. The differences between the two reports are in the expenses and the "Net Assets Released from Restrictions." The adjusted report is the one acceptable according to GAAP.

When comparing the two examples, you may notice that the $15,490 in net asset release is the sum of the books and scholarships expenses on the other report. Therefore, the nonprofit spent the money but it was "credited" by the restricted net asset.

To facilitate accounting, some nonprofits implement a policy of recognizing restricted funds as unrestricted when the expenses are expected to happen during the same year. Instead of the nonprofit recognizing a temporarily restricted revenue and then releasing it throughout the year, accounting just recognizes the money as unrestricted and document it to be able to show its release in the "official" financial statements.

Chart of Accounts

The chart of accounts should be able to accommodate many net assets, inter-fund receivables/payables, financial, grant, and 990 reporting. Actually, many organizations set up their chart of accounts following the line items in the 990, which is usually good enough. However, nonprofits may receive grant funds where the grantor requires a certain account setup that needs to be followed.

When setting up accounts, segments must be considered carefully. For instance, a "1" in the beginning or ending of an account may point to the account belonging to an unrestricted fund. A "2" would mean the account is temporarily restricted. Then, two digits could be used to identify each temporarily restricted fund—01 would be Scholarship, 02 would be Construction, 03 would be Special books, etc. A restricted account for construction donations would look like this: 2-02-xxxx-xxx.

Some nonprofits' charts of accounts are not set up properly, with disastrous results. Unrestricted and restricted funds should be identified at the chart of accounts level, not just in reporting. I have seen a nonprofit with a chart of accounts with no easily identifiable temporarily restricted funds. Instead, the nonprofit staff had to select accounts manually for reporting. Problems started when certain accounts were being "forgotten" and fund balances were incorrect. Note that if a nonprofit uses a "project" or "grant" accounting module, or "class" setup, the chart of accounts can be more general since a lot of information is picked up by the module or class.

As expected, the common reporting needs of nonprofits require the chart of accounts to be multidimensional and to allow for easy reporting by program, department, grant, funds, etc. Next is an excerpt of a chart of accounts.

Nonprofit organization A has three programs: Therapy, Tutorial Services, and Child Care. It receives funds from a government grant and from public donations.

The organization uses the setup XXXX-YYYY

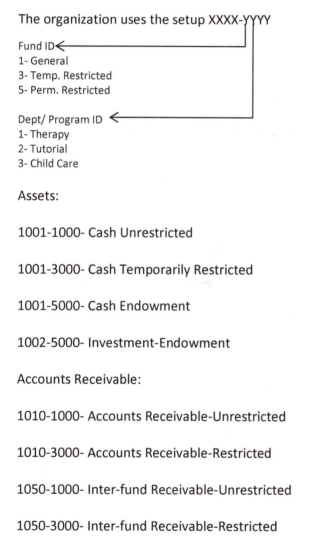

Fund ID
1- General
3- Temp. Restricted
5- Perm. Restricted

Dept/ Program ID
1- Therapy
2- Tutorial
3- Child Care

Assets:

1001-1000- Cash Unrestricted

1001-3000- Cash Temporarily Restricted

1001-5000- Cash Endowment

1002-5000- Investment-Endowment

Accounts Receivable:

1010-1000- Accounts Receivable-Unrestricted

1010-3000- Accounts Receivable-Restricted

1050-1000- Inter-fund Receivable-Unrestricted

1050-3000- Inter-fund Receivable-Restricted

Liabilities:

2000-1000- Accounts Payable-Unrestricted

2000-3000- Accounts Payable-Restricted

2050-1000- Inter-fund Payable-Unrestricted

2050-3000- Inter-fund Payable-Restricted

Net Assets/Funds:

3000-1000- General/Unrestricted Fund

3000-3000- Temporarily Restricted Fund

3000-5000- Permanently Restricted Fund

Revenues:

4000-1000- General Contributions

4090-1000- Net Assets Released from Restriction (*usually a credit*)

4090-3000- Net Assets Released from Restriction (*usually a debit*)

4100-1100- Fees for Services-Therapy

4100-1200- Fees for Services-Tutorial

4100-1300- Fees for Services-Child Care

4200-3100- Contributions-Therapy-Restricted

4200-3200- Contributions-Tutorial-Restricted

4200-3300- Contributions-Child Care-Restricted

4300-1001- Annual Fundraising Event

4301-1001- Contra revenue account to show donor's direct costs of event

Expenses:

6000-1000- Salary-Administrative

6000-1100- Salary-Therapy

6000-1200- Salary-Tutorial

6000-1300- Salary – Child Care

6010-1000- Telephone-Administrative

6010-1100- Telephone-Therapy

6010-1200- Telephone-Tutorial

(Note that all expenses come out of unrestricted fund.)

Using this system, reports can be generated by fund, program, type of account, etc. The last two digits of the second segment can identify different fundraising events and special programs within each department. For instance, within the therapy department, we could separate therapy for teens and therapy for adults. The more detailed the chart of account is, the more flexible it is in reporting. (Therapy for teens and adults may also be segregated by using "classes," if available).

✓ **Grant revenue is usually restricted and should be incorporated in the chart of accounts and/or grant modules or classes.**

If this organization receives a $1,000 donation for any purpose, then account 4000-1000 is credited. This account closes into General Fund balance/net asset- 3000-1000.

When someone donates $2,000 to be used in therapy to start next year, then account 4200-3100-Contributions-Therapy-Restricted is credited. This account closes into the 3000-3000-Temporarily Restricted Fund. This may be the case also if the $2,000 is to cover a specific type of therapy not yet available.

To summarize:

- All income/expense accounts like XXXX-1YYY- close into 3000-1000

- All income/expense accounts like XXXX-3YYY- close into 3000-3000

- All income/expense accounts like XXXX-5YYY- close into 3000-5000

The chart of accounts should be set up for users to compile data for both financials and 990 tax returns along with any other reports, such as for donors or sales taxes. There is a fine line between having an effective chart of accounts and one that is cumbersome to maintain.

Many nonprofits have issues with their chart of accounts about which management may not be aware. Sometimes managers decide to keep the original chart of accounts, changing instead the reporting system. I highly recommend going to the heart of the problem and changing the chart of accounts, instead of playing around with reporting, which could miss new accounts.

<u>**Summary**</u>

Financial statements can be prepared using the cash or accrual method of accounting, with the accrual style being more accepted because it includes accounts receivable and payable. The accrual method is recognized by GAAP for financial statements compilations. Nonprofits' "official" financial statements include net assets, also known as funds, and releases from restrictions. To keep it all organized, a sensible chart of accounts is required.

Additionally, nonprofits present net assets in three different "buckets": unrestricted, temporarily restricted, and permanently restricted. The unrestricted net asset is used for operations, presenting all if not most of the expenses, while the temporarily restricted net asset accumulates information about revenues restricted by donors. The permanent restricted net asset is employed to handle long-term assets, such as endowments.

5

Revenue Types and Issues

"May your charity increase as much as your wealth."

Proverb

A ll businesses must obtain revenues to survive and pay their bills. Unlike for-profit businesses where revenue streams come from sales or billings, nonprofit organizations' revenues typically come from donations, grants, fundraising activities, and non-donation items, such as tuitions. These different types of income need to be reported separately, creating a very detailed and complex accounting situation.

Depending on the nature of the revenue, nonprofits may classify them as "contributions" or as "exchange." ASC 958-605 (formerly known as FAS 116) guides the nonprofit treatment of revenues, which may be a bit tricky at times. The basic idea is that if a donor receives something in return for a payment, part of or the entire amount may not be a donation/contribution.

Contribution or Exchange

A contribution may be defined as a voluntary unconditional transfer of assets where the donor receives no correlated benefit. It is a straight gift. Donors may impose restrictions on the contribution, but they are not beneficiaries of the restrictions, not receiving anything of value in return. As far as accounting is concerned, nonprofits recognize contributions as revenues when received or pledged.

The other type of revenue, exchange, is a contribution where the donor receives something valuable in return. This could be a fee for seminars or tuition for school. In this situation, the people receive something in return, similar to a for-profit business sale. Exchanges may or may not be recognized as revenues when received or pledged, depending on the situation.

For example, an organization received a straight donation from a business for $10,000 for any purpose. The same organization also received another check for $10,000 to pay for seminar fees. The nonprofit will classify these two checks differently:

- o The first check has no strings attached and is considered to be a contribution or a donation.

- o The second check has strings attached; the donor will receive something in return. The payment is an exchange, not a donation.

The first check, a contribution, will be shown on the Statement of Activities (Income Statement of nonprofits) as part of the unrestricted net assets. If the donor sets up any restrictions on the money, then the nonprofit would present it under the temporarily or permanently restricted net asset column.

The second check, the exchange, will be shown on the Statement of Position (Balance Sheet of nonprofits) as part of the unrestricted net asset deferred revenue-deposits. Once the seminar happens, the nonprofit recognizes the revenue as unrestricted on the Statement of Activities. No release accounts are used with exchanges. Issues pointing to an exchange situation are:

- Financial penalties if the terms of the agreement are not met
- Donor specifies the place and time of the program
- There is a possibility of a "profit margin"
- Donor receives direct benefits from the organization
- The nonprofit offers a specific program, rather than doing activities that would benefit the public in general

Summary of contributions and exchange treatment:

Type of revenue	When received for future use:
Donation	Revenue-Temporarily Restricted Net Asset
Exchange	Deferred Revenue, like in for-profit
Type of revenue	When activity happens:
Donation	Release of Temporarily Restricted Net Assets
Exchange	Debit Deferred Revenue and credit regular Revenue

In general, most grants received from private foundations and other donors are considered contributions, while government grants are exchange transactions. However, in some cases, private grants can be exchange transactions or a combination of both

Donations of Cash, Checks, and Credit Cards

Many donors give donations in the form of cash, checks, or credit cards. Such gifts are recognized for the amount given, so when a nonprofit receives a check for $100, accounting recognizes it as an increase in cash and as a type of revenue. If the money is for general use, then the unrestricted revenue is booked, while if the purpose is for a specific program, the temporarily restricted revenue is used and released later on.

Since cash and checks are easy to lose, they must be deposited in the bank right away. Many banks allow for online deposit of checks, making this process easier. Pictures of checks can be taken from inside the banks' app on iPhone or iPad, making it the perfect deposit solution when the nonprofit receives only a few checks a week. Payments in cash must be discouraged whenever possible to avoid the risk of loss and misappropriation.

Dealing with donations can be a problem in times of appeal or other fundraising events. A strategy should be in place for the donations to be put in a safe place ASAP. I have been to events where envelopes containing pledges, checks, and cash were thrown in the trash by mistake. Have a group of people responsible for picking all types of donations and put them in a safe place right away. It is a good idea to have more than one person counting the cash before it is deposited.

In addition, before any campaign or marketing material goes out, someone from the accounting staff should look at it. I have seen marketing materials going out without a space for credit card expiration dates, creating confusion and loss of income. Accountants are usually detailed-oriented and would be able to catch these problems before it is too late.

Stock Donations

Nonprofits may receive stocks as donations, as many people donate stocks to nonprofits as part of a tax savings strategy. These are especially popular in December.

In order to safeguard the stocks or to cash them, an organization needs to work with a brokerage firm that holds the actual stocks, tracks or sell them. To handle this type of donation, many nonprofits have an investment committee deciding how to invest funds and monitor fund performance. These committees are traditionally conservative in their investment strategies.

Besides committees, many nonprofit organizations have policies about stock donations—some hold on to the stocks, others sell it right away, and still others leave the decisions to their brokers based on certain parameters or goals. The idea is to maximize the stock value.

The assessment of stock donations follows FASB 157 (ASC 820) regarding investments' valuation. This ASC includes guidance of alternative-type investments that are inherently riskier and may be part of the nonprofit's portfolio.

Overall, stock donations are booked as assets and nonprofits should:

1. Report at current fair value any equity investments that have readily determinable fair values; and

2. Show any gains or losses in the Statement of Activities, one of the standard financial statements.

Suppose stocks are given to fulfill pledge commitments. It is important to get the fair market value of the stock when given to verify if proceeds would fulfill the commitment or not. Actual funds received may be more or less than pledges. Donors will need to be contacted regarding directions on how to apply any surplus and/or how to pay outstanding commitments in full.

Nonprofits give receipts based on donated stock values when gifted for donors' tax returns. Any gains or losses, dividends, etc. are to be booked by organizations as investment transactions.

If securities were donated with no restrictions, any gains or losses are booked into the unrestricted fund. If the securities were given as restricted and the donor gave specific instructions on gains and losses, donor wishes should be followed. Realized and unrealized gains and losses are booked the year they happen and in the fund/net asset they belong to. Next is an example of a stock donation:

1- An organization receives an equity security valued at $30,000 in year 20X1

2- At fiscal year-end, the value of the security is $40,000

3- The organization sells the security for $43,000 in year 20X2

The security is booked as an investment. An unrealized gain of $10,000 is recognized at 20X1 year-end. In year 20X2, a realized gain of

$3,000 is recognized along with cash of $43,000.

Donations of stocks may be given as part of a permanent restricted fund. Endowments' income and gains/losses may be booked to temporarily restricted funds, unrestricted, or permanently restricted funds, depending on the donor's stipulation and local law.

Some endowments are specific about the type of investment to be held and managed, and the manner in which income, gains, and losses are to be applied. This avoids confusion later on. The more specific a donor is, the better the organization can account for the endowment. The UPMIFA law, promulgated by each state, must be followed for endowments and long-term gifts.

If a nonprofit receives significant stock donations and has the ability to influence a firm's financial and operating policies, then the equity method of accounting is to be used. This is handled the same way as if the nonprofit were a for-profit firm.

Pledges Receivable

Most nonprofit organizations are familiar with pledges. People, businesses, and foundations can make pledges to give in the future. Pledges are promises to give. Many times these promises are the results of a fundraising campaign or an appeal. Depending on the situation, the pledge could be for a general or specific purpose, such as a new child-care program. As far as accounting is concerned, general pledges are recognized in the unrestricted net assets, while the specific-purpose ones are classified as restricted net assets.

Pledges, both short-term and long-term, may be shown as "Pledges" or "Unconditional promises to give" on the Statement of Position.

✓ **All unconditional pledges are recorded as assets**.

For example, suppose a donor pledges $2,000 a year for five years as an unconditional gift. The pledge is booked as a receivable (asset) and as revenue on the date the nonprofit receives the pledge document. However, suppose there is a condition associated with a pledge. In that case, the nonprofit records the pledge only after the condition is met. If the condition is the occurrence of a major disaster in California, this pledge is conditional and the nonprofit should not record it. Once a disaster hits California, then the pledge may be valid.

Another example of a condition is when a firm matches donations made by employees. If an employee donates $10, the firm would also pay $10, matching the donor's amount. As the employee donates, the condition on the firm's pledge is lifted. Therefore, each time an employee pays, the nonprofit recognizes a matching pledge in the accounting books.

The wording of a pledge is crucial to determine when a promise is conditional or just restricted. The key word in conditional pledges is "if." Those are usually not recorded.

A pledge can be restricted to a certain time or event, such as for a reading program happening in the future. This type of pledge is restricted and unconditional as reflected by the words "when" or "what included in the promise, not "if." Restricted and unconditional pledges are recorded. Nonprofits recognize unconditional pledges with restrictions as part of the temporarily restricted net asset. Sometimes donors can change their minds, and instead of funding program A, they decide to fund program B. To support any changes, nonprofits should keep proper documentation.

Beware: Not all promises are pledges. For example, if a person notifies an organization that he is including the nonprofit in his will, this is not a pledge and is not recognized in the accounting books. The same situation exists if someone promises to pay a certain amount twenty years in the future—it is not a pledge. In both cases, donors can easily change their minds; circumstances can change, making the promises hard to keep. Nonprofits should use common sense in this area.

As promises to give in the future, pledges may not be all collectible. Most organizations are not going to sue to collect promised amounts because of PR issues. Therefore, by its nature, pledges are riskier than regular accounts receivable. A pledge due in a year is less risky than a pledge due in two or more years since a lot can happen in a year or longer.

Because there is a risk of default on pledges receivable, an Allowance for Uncollectible Pledges account is used. It may be set up and adjusted every year based on history. If an organization experiences 15 percent of uncollectible pledges, this percentage can be used. It is the same concept as the Allowance for Uncollectible Receivables in the for-profit world.

Nonprofits could have pledges payable in installments; for example, a pledge of $25,000 payable at $5,000 a year for five years. FASB requires nonprofits to discount long-term pledges to present value using a reasonable percentage. The discount is amortized as in the nonprofit world. FASB ASC 820-10 (FASB 157) also relates to this topic to be sure organizations evaluate pledges in a fair and acceptable manner.

✓ **Government and other grants are not pledges.**

Organizations must have pledge documents in writing whenever possible. If a donor does not want to acknowledge the pledge, a thank you letter confirming the pledge is a good idea. The letter can be simple and brief, but should leave no doubt about the existence of the pledge.

Many times big donors want to keep their donations and personal information private. To this end, nonprofits implement proper care so that the donor is acknowledged, donations are recorded, and the donor's identity is kept private. Nonprofit donor databases need to be kept secure. Only a few people should possess access to the donors' records. A nonprofit organization I worked with had famous celebrities donating significant amounts of money, and they did not want their names, email addresses or other information available. Therefore, instead of putting the real names and information in the database, the organization used the names "Anonymous 1," "Anonymous 2," etc. The nonprofit kept the real names and personal information under lock and key in a file cabinet accessible only by a couple of people.

Fundraising Events

Most nonprofit organizations conduct fundraising events to raise money for operations or certain programs. Often nonprofits hold annual fundraising events, such as mailing campaigns, marathons, golf tournaments, dinners, and galas to raise money for general use.

FASB Accounting Standards Codification (ASC) Document 958 provides guidance in presenting fundraising revenues and costs on financial statements. Other pronouncements may also apply, depending on the type of event and donations.

Proceeds and expenses associated with these events are usually booked into the unrestricted/general fund. However, if the fundraising event is for a specific program or for something to happen in the following year, then revenues from the event are considered to be temporarily restricted.

The difference between the amount paid and the fair value of the benefits received by the donor is recognized as a contribution. For example, if a donor pays $200 for a dinner that is worth $150, the difference of $50 is a contribution, a "real" donation. The costs of such dinner, as benefits, are known as "Direct Donor Costs." These are not fundraising costs; rather, they are classified as program expenses on financial statements. They could be costs of a dinner, refreshments, rent of a restaurant, etc.

Besides costs, nonprofits should know the fair market value (FMV) of each event and auction item. Why? Because the difference between the donation and the items received in exchange is tax deductible to the donor. Nonprofits must provide information about FMV to event attendees, usually disclosed on the event ticket and on auction information sheets.

✓ **The Direct Donor benefit cost is based on actual costs, while the exchange portion is based on fair market value.**

Fundraising activities are presented on the "Statement of Activities" (Income Statement of nonprofits). Special events are shown separately along with the direct donor benefit costs associated with fundraising events. Actually, organizations may choose among three methods for recording and presenting direct benefit costs on financial statements. They are:

○ Option 1: Display the costs of direct benefits to donors as a separate line item deducted from the special event gross revenues.

○ Option 2: Display gross revenues in the revenue section and the direct benefits costs as part of "other programs" or "supporting services." Allocation of the expenses may also be necessary.

○ Option 3: Display both the contribution and the exchange portion as special event revenue. The benefits costs are deducted from the exchange number.

According to the IRs, certain nonprofits need to file 990-Schedule G to give details on all gaming and fundraising activities. The schedule requires information regarding gross receipts and contributions for each event along with expenses. It also inquires about fundraisers payments and states where fundraising events have happened.

Other considerations regarding fundraising include the following:

o   Be sure the fundraising event really brings money in. Sometimes fundraisers do not account for all expenses included in the event as many expenses come in after the event. Nonprofits must review fundraising activities to make sure they are indeed bringing in more than they are spending. An event bringing in $100 net of all expenses may not be worth all the work.

o   Sales/Excise taxes- Each state has its own rules and laws regarding fundraising. Some states tax auctions, while other states tax all fundraising and still others offer exemptions for nonprofits. Taxes decrease revenues and, in some cases, they can be substantial.

o   If nonprofits use credit card or third parties in fundraising, they must consider processing charges. The organization may pay 2 to 3 percent plus as a surcharge for each donation or purchase using a credit card. When budgeting for events, take into consideration these charges.

Many times organizations combine fundraising with programs or with management/general. When this happens, a reasonable allocation of expenses may be used. This situation is also known as "Joint Costs," discussed in detail in another chapter.

Donation Receipts

It is always a good idea to give receipts to donors, especially when the donation is in cash. Besides being a good procedure, the IRS also has receipt requirements that nonprofits must comply with.

The basic concept is that nonprofits should give receipts for donations over $250. As the IRS does not require a specific receipt form to be filled out, the receipt could be a letter, a postcard, an e-mail message, or a form created for this purpose with the name of the organization clearly shown. It is not necessary to add Social Security or tax ID numbers to the receipts. Per the IRS (www.irs.gov), receipts for such donations should include the following components:

- Name of organization
- Amount of cash contribution
- Description (but not the value) of non-cash contribution
- Statement that no goods or services were provided in return for the contribution if that is the case.
- Description and good-faith estimate of the value of goods or services, if any, that an organization provided in return for the contribution.
- Statement that goods or services, if any, that an organization provided in return for the contribution consisted entirely of intangible religious benefits, if it was the case.

An example of such a receipt would be: "Thank you for your contribution of $450 to ABC Nonprofit made in the name of its Special Scholarship program. No goods or services were provided in exchange for your contribution."

Besides the $250 threshold, if a donor receives something in return for a contribution of $75 or more, the organization must give a receipt as well, called a "Written Disclosure." The idea is that only a part of the "donation" is a "real" donation or contribution, not the entire amount. This statement must:

- Inform a donor that the deductible amount of the contribution for federal tax purposes is limited to the excess of money contributed by the donor over the value of goods or services provided by the organization.

- Provide a donor with a good-faith estimate of the fair market value of the goods or services.

In practice, as mentioned earlier, nonprofits include this language on event tickets and other materials, making the disclosure obvious and clear. It is common to see tickets for special events indicating the fair market value of the event. It seems a bit tacky, but organizations do it for a good reason.

A penalty of $10 per contribution up to $5,000 per fundraising event or mailing applies when nonprofits do not meet the written disclosure requirement. The IRS could abate this penalty if the nonprofit can show reasonable cause for this failure.

Sometimes, organizations send donors' receipts by January 31 of the following year. This receipt lists all donations for the year, helping donors to file their tax returns. Computerized systems help to create these yearly statement-receipts, but this means that someone must have entered detailed data in the software, which can be time-consuming and costly. So, usually larger nonprofits only provide this service.

Beware: Donors may ask for donation receipts, when no donation really occurred. I have seen parents asking for donation receipts for tuition paid on a school that was part of a nonprofit. Receipts were provided, but for tuition, not donations. Nonprofits do not want to participate in tax-evasion schemes but at the same time, they do not want to upset a member or a donor. Clear procedures should be in place to avoid confusion and ill feelings. Sometimes the best approach is to give people general receipts with descriptions of the transactions.

CEOs, presidents, or executive directors may want to make the receipt more individualized and prefer to handwrite personal notes. They could use pads for receipts with the IRS information required as footers and handwrite a personal note in the blank space above. This way the donor receives a personalized thank you letter and an IRS receipt in one-step.

Make sure to save copies of receipts. Donors can lose original receipts, and the nonprofit will need to give them copies. This happens all the time, especially at tax time during the months of March and April.

As a general comment, organizations' staff should refrain from giving tax advice to donors. Nonprofits are not in the business of providing expert tax advice. They can provide information regarding an event, as required, but not beyond this level of information. Each tax situation is different; a cost may be deductible on one person's tax return, but it may not be deductible on another's.

In-Kind Contributions- Service

Volunteers, often the soul of an organization, contribute many services—from clerical work to executive positions—giving the nonprofit culture and personality. Without volunteer work, many organizations would have closed a long time ago.

How does an organization account for volunteer work? Clearly, there is a value to it, but no money changes hands. No salaries or wages are paid. SFAS 116 used to provide guidance on this topic. Now, FASB ASC-580- 310, 360, and 605, along with ASC 958-605, give accounting rules for this type of contributions. Following such guidance, nonprofits recognize contributed services only if the services:

- Create or enhance non-financial assets, and
- Are provided by individuals possessing specialized skills, and would need to be purchased if they were not provided by donation.

Typically, specialized skills providers include accountants, architects, doctors, electricians, nurses, plumbers, and teachers. Doctors volunteering at a summer camp for kids with disabilities would qualify for service donations. A CPA doing an organization's tax returns free of charge would qualify as well.

The basis for assigning value to the services must be reasonable. $100-$150 per hour would work for doctors or CPAs, for instance. The value may also be the fair market value of the asset improvement resulting from the in-kind services.

✓ **Fundraising volunteers are not considered in the accounting books.**

In most cases, donated services are recognized in the unrestricted fund and have no effect on the bottom line since they affect both revenue and expenses. (The entry is to debit in-kind services expense and credit in-kind services revenue) However, in some instances, because of the nature of the donation, nonprofits could capitalize the expenses, as in the case of volunteers working on building improvements, software programs, or other assets.

Keep track of volunteers with time sheets and logs. Also treat them very well; they are promoting the organization and providing needed services. Many organizations would not provide the goods and services if it were not for the volunteers. Note that, details on contributed services, such as fair values and allocation methods, are parts of the "Disclosure Notes" at the end of official financial statements.

Although services may be recognized in the nonprofit's financial statements, the value of such work cannot be deducted in individuals' tax returns. Donors may take a special mileage deduction and expenses related to the donated work, but they cannot deduct the value of actual services, such as lawyers' fees. A lawyer or other professional can deduct the costs of donated paper and supplies, for example, but not their hourly fees.

The IRS does not allow the reporting of donated services, only donated goods. However, nonprofits can add the value of such services as a narrative on 990- Schedule O.

Remember to include volunteers on insurance policies. Volunteers can misbehave, steal, or fall down the stairs, and the organization is liable for these events. There are policies specifically for volunteers that may be considered by many organizations.

In-Kind Contributions-Donations of Things

Many people and businesses donate clothes, food, furniture, jewelry, equipment, etc. to an organization. Some even donate real estate and inventory goods.

Nonprofits must be careful about what they accept as donations. For instance, a donor could donate a building and land to an organization. Should the nonprofit accept them? Not until building inspectors and other professionals give the property a clean bill of health or disclose what needs to be done to the building.

With certain real estate donations, it is possible that a major asbestos cleanup is needed, or maybe there is a hazardous material underneath the soil, and the "gift" can become quite expensive to maintain. Certain major gifts may cause unforeseen raises in insurance premiums, which might be prohibitive to the organization along with too costly maintenance and fees. Because of the risks involved with large donations, usually the Executive Director and/or G&A personnel are involved in making decisions about the situation. In addition, policies and procedures should cover this type of contributions.

FASB ASC 820-10 (FASB 157) provides guidance on how to measure fair value consistently for goods and services. In the case of goods, the nonprofits should evaluate the products properly, following a level methodology, similar to the evaluation of investments. Next are the levels expected to be used in this situation:

- Level 1- Item is evaluated based on quoted prices in the market for identical assets.

- Level 2- Item is evaluated based on like-kind comparison. For example, the fair market value of a building could be derived by reviewing selling prices at various similar buildings in comparable locations.

- o Level 3- Item is valued based on "unobservable" data, such as donor's estimation of fair value.

Anything of value, such as jewelry, or any good valued at $5,000 or more should be professionally inspected, not just for insurance purposes, but for IRS compliance as well. The IRS procedures are:

- ➢ Donor fills out Form 8283 upon donation of the gift

- ➢ Nonprofit management fills out Part IV of the Form 8283 upon receipt of the gift

- ➢ If the nonprofit sells the gift within three years, the organization files Form 8282 with a copy sent to the donor

Like in-kind services, nonprofits present in-kind goods in detail in the notes of the official financial statements, including information on donor type, nature, fair market value, valuation method used, and allocations of the goods.

The organization is not required to accept every gift and is not expected to value donations, as gift valuation is usually the donor's responsibility. The nonprofit can give a receipt with a detailed description of the items donated with not much about the dollar value of the donation.

✓ **Unlike in-kind services, in-kind goods are reported on the tax return 990.**

Organizations should keep track of all in-kind goods, such as donations of furniture, computer systems, etc. Since no cash changes hands, it is easy to forget such goods, but they should be input in the accounting system as revenue and asset/ expense.

Donations of Art/Museum Pieces

Donations of antiquities and works of art are a different class of donations. These are pieces with historical or artistic value and are:

- Used for public exhibition, research, or education, as a public service and not for financial gain

- Safeguarded, protected, and cared for

- Protected by organization policy to buy more pieces for the collection, in case these items are sold

Nonprofits should evaluate the maintenance costs of museum/art items, such climate controls, burglar alarms/cameras, security guards, and other expenses that can be substantial. Nonprofits need to possess enough resources to safeguard the valuable pieces.

Existing collections and any other new gifts should be re-evaluated yearly. Some items could have been moved out of the organization or suffered damage. Nonprofits often update their insurance policies to cover any decreases or increases in value, new pieces, etc.

Nonprofits have a choice to capitalize the museum/art pieces or not. Either way, the organization needs to be consistent in dealing with accounting for these items. When a nonprofit capitalizes a collection, it records it as an asset and as revenue. Collections are presented on a separate line item in the Statement of Financial Position (the nonprofit version of a Balance Sheet).

✓ **Capitalized collections are not depreciated.**

Split Interest Agreements

Donors could give nonprofits benefits that are shared with other parties. This type of gift, involving split interest agreement, often involves more than one nonprofit or a nonprofit and other parties. This setup might include a fixed payment going back to the donor until his/her death. In addition, these agreements may allow for cash inflows to the nonprofit on a long-term basis.

Split interest agreements may be revocable or not. This difference is important because revocable split interest agreements are usually not recognized as revenues by the nonprofit, while irrevocable ones are. Trusts may be involved in these deals, which can be complicated. These agreements are commonly known as the following:

- Charitable lead trusts—Nonprofit is named as beneficiary

- Perpetual trusts held by third parties—Only income earned is distributed to the nonprofit, not the assets (corpus) held in trust

- Charitable remainder trusts—When trust terms are terminated, the nonprofit receives the remaining assets

- Charitable gift annuities—Assets are held by the organization and an annuity is set up for the third party

- Pooled (life) income funds—Investment based on life insurance policies and funding. The donor receives income until death, when the nonprofit gets the full value of the investment

The revenue recognition issues go back to FASB ASC 820-10 (FASB 157), involving the mortality of donor and the risk involved with credit ratings. Revenue valuation of a split interest agreement is based on the fair market value of the asset transferred, including any liabilities.

Generally, nonprofits categorize split interest agreement amounts as temporarily restricted because of the implicit time restrictions of the gift, but donor's wish may override this classification.

Many nonprofits implement a "Gift Acceptance Policy or Committee" to oversee these types of gifts because they can be complex. Nonprofits should be sure the deal:

- Is legal

- Complies with the acceptable risk

- Is in compliance with state laws and regulations

- Is the type of asset that has been approved

- Is in compliance with the minimum gift amount

- Is in compliance with the minimum age for immediate and deferred gifts

- Follows industry standards

- Is doable as far as gift designations are honored

Details of split interest agreements are presented in the "Disclosure Notes" at the end of the official financial statements, including changes in value, summary of the terms, and the basis used for valuation.

Summary

Nonprofit organizations receive many types of revenues, such as cash/check donations, grants, and pledges that may or may not be collectible. They also receive in-kind donations of services and things and are parties on split interest agreements.

Not all revenues are the same, even though they seem similar. Besides IRS receipting rules, nonprofit management needs to analyze the types and restrictions to classify the funds properly in the accounting books and tax forms.

Sheila Shanker

6

Government Grants

"The object of government in peace and in war is not the glory of rulers or of races, but the happiness of the common man."

Lord William Beveridge (1879-1963)

The government's job is about governing, protecting, and helping people as the saying above indicates. However, governments are too large to provide certain services to many communities. This is where nonprofits come into play. They provide services governments cannot perform as well and as efficiently.

Government grants often involve large sums of money, and grantors want assurances that nonprofits spend the funds properly. Such government grants can come from state, city, county, or federal sources. In this chapter, we will concentrate on federal U.S. grants, although oftentimes federal funds are passed –through states first.

Governmental grants include their own language, rules, and reporting requirements. They can be very complex. For instance, some grants pay organizations ahead of time, while others require nonprofits to file reports before funds are released for reimbursement. Additionally, some grants pay nonprofits based on head count and not on expenses incurred.

✓ **Grants are not repaid. They are payments for goods and services provided.**

A comprehensive listing of government grants is available at the Catalog of Federal Financial Assistance at https://www.cfda.gov/. This catalog lists all available federal grants and is updated often. The number of federal grants given by top agencies in December 2014 was:

503 Department of Health and Human Services

270 Department of the Interior

261 Department of Agriculture

135 Department of Justice

120 Department of Education

This CFDA website allows many ways to look for grants: by keyword, agency, beneficiary type, etc. Each grant has a specific number and purpose. Development staff could search for grants available, requirements, and the application process. Another good website for federal government grants is www.grants.gov. It contains links to grants, help in writing grant proposals, and other useful resources.

Many nonprofits function as "pass-through" entities to other nonprofits. For instance, an organization receives funds for research and then distributes them to appropriate institutions. The organization does not do the research, but gives the money to others involved with specific research interests.

✓ **Pass-through organizations should be paid for administrative costs.**

It is important for organizations with pass-through funds to get enough money to manage the grants coming in and going out. Not all money is pass-through; some funds must stay within the organization to cover direct and indirect costs associated with the management of such grants.

Once a grant is awarded, the nonprofit can register and use the System for Award Management (SAM) that consolidates many rules and functions. This system is at https://www.sam.gov.

Sometimes government entities make nonprofits the intermediary, inadvertently. A real-life example: A school used to receive government funds to distribute to disabled students every month. The government agency should have mailed the checks to the families' addresses, but instead, it sent the money to the school. The situation created an administrative burden for the school, which was not getting anything for this work. When the school started to return the checks, the agency began to send the money directly to the families. Point of this vignette: Nonprofits should not do free work for the government.

An interesting byproduct of a nonprofit being funded by various government agencies, is that their accountants become specialists in each grant because of the complexity involved in each contract, including specific reporting and different ways to obtain funds. Compliance issues, deadlines, and issues related to each grant reporting can be different.

This specialization can help accountants get jobs in other nonprofits or businesses that receive the same type of funding. As expected, when organizations need to hire new accounting staff, experience with certain grants or government agencies are seen as a major plus to the applicant.

Financial Management

As of December 2014, nonprofits must comply with a "Super OMB Circular," also known as the "Omni Circular." Its official name is "OMB Uniform Guidance: Administrative Requirements, Cost Principles, and Audit Requirements for Federal Awards." This guidance will replace a few circulars, such as A-110, A-122, and A-133, streamlining the process of acquiring and maintaining federal grants while trying to avoid duplication and waste. You can find the full text of this circular at https://www.federalregister.gov/articles/2013/12/26/2013-30465/uniform-administrative-requirements-cost-principles-and-audit-requirements-for-federal-awards.

The new Omni Circular specifies the information required from federal agencies when announcing funding opportunities and evaluating nonprofits as recipients. Some issues government agencies need to consider would be:

- Organization fiscal stability
- Quality of management and systems
- Audit reports
- Performance history

If the federal agency or pass-through entity identifies risks involved with an organization, it is likely to require additional reports and decide to use a reimbursement basis instead of advance funding. This means that no money would be provided in advance, but reported costs may be reimbursed by grantor after they are incurred.

To manage all grant deadlines and compliance requirements, many organizations set up summary worksheets or tables on each contract with specific details regarding requirements, reports, dates, etc. Instead of going through an entire contract to find an item, one could go to the summary, saving lots of time and effort. Nonprofits may also set up a calendar listing the deadlines for each grant contract. They might use computerized reminders to send out emails reminding managers of upcoming deadlines and other compliance issues that can cost nonprofits a lot of money.

The major information source for federal grants, the Super or Omni Circular is clear about the fiscal expectations for grantees, including requirements as the following:

> ➤ The ability to identify each grant received and expenses associated with each grant

> ➤ The resources to provide accurate, current, and complete financial reporting as required

> ➤ The maintenance of proper records

> ➤ Appropriate internal controls

> ➤ Written procedures for allowable costs and grant payments

> ➤ Comparison of expenditures with budget amounts for each federal award

---

If a nonprofit is not on the accrual basis, but the granting agency requires accrual reporting, the organization does not need to convert its accounting books to accrual, only the grant reports. This can be done by adjusting the report numbers as needed.

Federal grantors want organizations to spend federal money right away with reimbursement being the preferred funding method. Nonprofits first spend the money and then request "drawdowns" as reimbursements. These reimbursements may present cash flow problems, though. For instance, billings sent out at the beginning of January are usually paid in February, which is not too bad; however, I have witnessed very late payments (more than four months late) because the nonprofit did not provide the government with proper reports online.

Often, online reports are the preferred method for reporting funds received and spent. If nonprofits do not file the reports by a certain date, the government does not release funds. Additionally, if the reports have errors or omissions, funding is likely to be delayed. Grant payments may also be held back when the required reports about program results and costs are not provided, or when only one of these reports is submitted.

In spite of grant payment delays, nonprofits must have healthy cash flows to pay expenses to be reimbursed in the future. Some bills may wait, while others, such as payroll, must be paid in a timely fashion. Some organizations use proceeds from program fees or special events to cover these liabilities. Others utilize bank lines of credit to provide the required cash flow and remain afloat.

Another issue organizations must deal with is the risk of funding cuts due to government budgets constraints. Therefore, they must have a "Plan B" that may involve cuts in administration, programs, or fundraising costs. Maybe some people could work part time instead of full time, for example, in case of funding cuts.

A big risk involved with grants is the noncompliance with terms of the agreement. I worked in a medical-related nonprofit where the therapist employed did not have all the education and experience required for the position, as required in the contract. The organization had a $100,000 reduction in its grant for the following year, which was material, forcing it to eliminate another program to absorb the cut. All individuals involved in a government-funded program, not just finance personnel, should know the details of the contract, including required particulars about personnel education and experience. Human resources department should know of these issues along with program managers.

When a nonprofit receives advances and/or has $120,000 in federal money, it should deposit the money in insured, preferably interest-bearing, bank accounts. The government does not want its money deposited in financial institutions that may be seen as risky.

In addition, if nonprofits earn interest of $500 or less, they can use the money to defray costs. However, in case the interest is more than $500, nonprofits must send the funds to the grantor. Check your grant agreement carefully regarding this topic. The idea here is to minimize the chances for losses and waste.

According the regulations, the annual and final reports requesting funds should include a certification, signed by an authorized official, which reads:

"By signing this report, I certify to the best of my knowledge and belief that the report is true, complete, and accurate, and the expenditures, disbursements and cash receipts are for the purposes and objectives set forth in the terms and conditions of the federal award. I am aware that any false, fictitious, or fraudulent information, or the omission of any material fact, may subject me to criminal, civil or administrative penalties for fraud, false statements, false claims or otherwise. (U.S. Code Title 18, Section 1001 and Title 31, Sections 3729-3730 and 3801-3812)."

Grant Budgets

Usually, nonprofits' grant proposals include budget numbers that are carefully considered, showing a realistic plan for the organization. These numbers are classified as direct and indirect and may be negotiated with the federal agency.

Once a contract is approved, it includes final budget numbers for one or more years. However, errors can happen and unexpected things occur, such as major changes in scope of services, calling for changes in the budget numbers. Such changes may be allowed, depending on grantor and situation.

Grant budget line items may also include some flexibility. If a budget has five lines within the administrative section, for instance, the total of administrative expenses may be considered, not each line. Suppose a nonprofit has an expense of $50 in postage-Administration to be reimbursed by a grant. The organization used up all the postage line item in the budget. However, this nonprofit has a line for supplies that still has $500 left. Depending on the grant contract, the organization could get the $50 reimbursed from supplies, even though the postage line is paid in full.

Usually, grantors provide nonprofits with templates and other assistance in developing budgets. Narratives and explanations are also part of the budget process—not just numbers. Oftentimes the accounting department must work with programs to assemble a report that meets both the quantitative and description/explanations sections.

To assist in grant budgeting and compliance, nonprofits' fiscal systems must be implemented to segregate revenues and expenses by grant, so that the individual reports can be generated easily. A grant module might be used by accounting to input and maintain grant budget numbers. Unlike regular accounting software, this module does not close every year, offering a layer of flexibility to the process. Some programs allow for notes, comments and can even calculate and apply overhead allocations, saving a lot of time.

When nonprofits use such software, their staff must enter each revenue and expense with the regular accounts plus a grant module code. This can improve reporting and management of grants, but it may increase the workload in the finance department, creating delays in processing accounts payable.

For example, if a nonprofit receives a bill for supplies, the staff needs to know not only the proper expense account, but also the program and grant classification. This is particularly important when a nonprofit has a program funded by more than one grant. Because of the cost and extra-work required with grant modules, usually only large organizations have been using them.

✓ **Assets purchased with federal funds do not need to be insured, unless specifically mentioned in the grant contract.**

Cost Principles

The federal grant cost principles are similar to the GAAP cost principles, but they are not the same. While administrative costs are typically indirect costs on both grant and GAAP bases, the idea of "allowable" costs does not exist with GAAP. Another difference is in vocabulary. The word "cost" is used in grants, but the word "expense" is employed with GAAP. They basically mean the same idea. Total costs of a federal grant comprise the following:

> ➤ Allowable direct costs plus

> ➤ Allowable indirect costs plus or minus

> ➤ Applicable credits

For costs to be allowed, they must be reasonable, consistent, documented, and mostly follow GAAP in accounting treatment. Not all costs are allowed in federally funded programs, and organizations must use common sense and fairness in spending federal grants. For instance, purchases of luxury goods are unnecessary and make no sense, especially when there are cheaper alternatives. Buying $200 wine bottles for the homeless is likely not to be allowable.

Allowable costs should be "allocable" to the program, i.e., the costs must be connected to the program, directly or indirectly. For example, if the executive director goes on a cruise for a vacation, federal grants will not cover its costs. Entertainment costs are not allowable, unless they are part of programs or were pre-approved or authorized in the budget. However, provisions exist to cover childcare, in an effort for federal grant recipients to be more "family-friendly." Therefore, nonprofits must review grant contract costs carefully.

According to many grant contracts, nonprofits cannot use certain vendors that are not permitted to participate in federally funded programs. The government keeps a list of companies that cannot be used for grant-funded projects at www.sam.gov. If a nonprofit uses any of them, the costs are not reimbursed.

Besides allowable costs, grant contracts mention credits, which could be discounts, insurance refunds, or error corrections decreasing costs. For instance, if a nonprofit receives a $100 rebate on a purchase using federal funding, the $100 should be netted against grant costs, decreasing them.

More than one grant may fund costs, making it important to allocate costs properly to each funding source. Typically, one grant cannot cover another grant's deficiency, unless it is pre-approved. "Double-dipping," i.e., receiving funds for the same expense from difference sources, is not acceptable.

A nonprofit usually submits a "Cost Allocation Plan" (CAP) identifying direct and indirect costs. This report shows past expenses to derive at a reasonable indirect cost rate. It can also be used when a nonprofit is new, or if it plans to start a new program. See an excerpt of this report next:

Schedule								
			DIRECT PROGRAMS AND ACTIVITIES					
A	B	C	D	E	F	G	H	I
ELEMENTS OF COSTS	FINANCIAL STATEMENT EXPENDITURES	ADJUSTMENTS/ UNALLOWABLE COSTS	SHELTER SERVICES	LITERACY PROGRAM	FOOD BANK	FUNDRAISING	(D)+(E)+(F)+(G) TOTAL DIRECT COSTS	INDIRECT COSTS
Salaries and wages	$357,789	0	$112,988	$88,934	$34,561	$12,767	$249,250	$108,539
Fringe benefits	$45,677	0	$25,987	$9,477	$3,564	$1,455	$40,483	$5,194
Subtotal labor & fringes	$403,466	0	$138,975	$98,411	$38,125	$14,222	$289,733	$113,733
Contractual services	$234,551	0	$55,434	$78,999	$34,158	$0	$168,591	$65,960
Depreciation/use allowance	$43,221	0	$0	$0	$0	$0	$0	$43,221

When certain costs are unusual or if questions arise on the appropriateness and allocation of certain expenses, nonprofits should negotiate with the government in advance whenever possible. The situation is the same with consolidations and other exemptions—all need approvals by a federal agency, and the sooner, the better. If a nonprofit spends questionable costs, it may end up not being reimbursed for these expenses. Better be safe than sorry.

Sometimes GAAP conflicts with grant accounting, such as in accounting for leases, where per GAAP the amounts should be capitalized, but if the nonprofit does that, it cannot be reimbursed according to many grant agreements. In situations like this, most nonprofits keep the internal accounting according to GAAP, and, in a worksheet, adjust the numbers to comply with grant reimbursement rules. This way the organization can be reimbursed for what it is due, while keeping back-up documentation, in case of any questions.

Direct and Indirect Costs

Direct costs

Direct costs are those easily identified with a specific program as nonprofits can assign these costs to a specific activity with great accuracy. Examples would be art supplies for an art program, art teachers who work only in one program, and mailing costs specific to the program.

Direct costs are often related to salaries of individuals working in specific programs. To capture this data, time sheets are used to identify people working on specific projects. Employees fill out online or paper time sheets that may be pre-coded for the work they currently perform. These numbers along with pay rates are transferred to the accounting system, separating each employee's pay to the proper program and grant. For example, salaries for people working in the art program will show up in separate reports from the ones working in childcare. Such data should be reviewed by supervisors to identify and correct any errors. It is good to know that the government pays for actual, not estimated direct costs.

Indirect Costs

Also known as overhead, these costs cannot be assigned to a program or funding source directly. Indirect costs must be related to the project grant, but cannot be readily identified. This can be similar to the GAAP indirect rate, but it is not exactly the same because grants may exclude some items and may have its own unique requirements. The Super Circular explains this area in detail.

✓ **State and other government grantor may define and calculate indirect costs differently.**

Unlike direct cost payments, the government pays indirect costs based on a percentage, which could be applied towards total direct costs (see Indirect Cost Rates section). If an organization reports $1,000 in direct expense, then, depending on the situation, 20 percent may be added to reflect overhead costs and the nonprofit would be paid $1,200.

As the Omni or Super Circular allows for a standard 10 percent indirect/overhead rate for all organizations receiving federal funds, nonprofits can apply this percentage to modified total direct costs (MTDC). This standard rate is set indefinitely without annual approvals. The MTDC includes all direct salaries and wages, appropriate fringe benefits, materials and supplies, services, travel, and sub-awards/sub-contracts, up to $25,000 for each one. MTDC excludes the following:

- Equipment (items over $5,000)

- Capital expenditures

- Charges for patient care

- Rental costs

- Tuition remission

- Scholarships

- Fellowships

- Participant support costs

- Sub-awards and sub-contracts in excess of the first $25,000

This simple setup may work well for many organizations. However, note that nonprofits are likely to show higher direct costs to get a larger base for the set percentage. For example, 10 percent of an MTDC of $15,000 is larger than 10 percent of MTDC of $11,000. The larger the MTDC, the better off the organization will be. Because of this situation, nonprofits may change the way some costs are derived, so they can be classified as direct. For example, organizations may give passwords to copy machine users to allocate copy expenses directly to certain projects.

Organizations can still negotiate rates with the government, especially large ones that implemented rates much higher than 10 percent. I have seen an indirect rate of 88 percent, so there is room for negotiations. Next is a summary of direct and indirect costs:

	Direct Costs	Indirect Costs
Characteristics	Easy to allocate to a program	Hard to allocate to a specific program
Grant funding	Paid based on actual direct costs	Paid based on an approved percentage or the standard 10%
Support	Actual bills and approved time sheets	Grant contract or approved CAP document

Indirect Cost Rates

As indirect cost rates can be substantial, many nonprofits negotiate with a government agency to increase their rates. The 10 percent default rate based on the Super Circular is not likely to work with large nonprofits, and many will need to negotiate higher rates.

For an indirect cost rate to be approved by a federal agency, the nonprofit must submit a document showing all expenses classified as direct or indirect and unallowable costs. This could be a CAP or other document showing past performance to estimate reasonableness for the rate.

The most popular method to allocate indirect costs is based on direct salaries, but many nonprofits use total costs as the basis for calculations. Once approved indirect cost rates may be extended up to four years without rate negotiations, subject to approval by the federal agency.

The idea is for indirect cost rates to distribute costs in a reasonable fashion. Next are some accepted ways to derive the indirect cost rate and do the allocations:

- o Simplified - All programs benefit from indirect costs to about the same degree. The idea is to implement one rate and go with it. This method is often used with small organizations that do not receive many federal grants.

- o Multiple - Indirect costs benefit a nonprofit organization's major functions in varying degrees. They accumulate in separate pools that hold similar characteristics and functions. Instead of calculating one rate, the organization gets multiple rates.

- o Special - Sometimes, factors preclude nonprofits from employing either the simplified or the multiple allocation types. Maybe the nature of the nonprofit work does not allow for such allocations. Alternatively, other issues, such as the physical site of the work, would not permit the usage of the other allocations. The nonprofit then may consider the special rate.

Once the rate is set, nonprofit staff needs to input only direct costs in the Internet-based reporting system of the federal government—the software applies the proper rate. If $300 is entered for reimbursement with an indirect rate of 50 percent, the nonprofit will be reimbursed $450. The larger the organization, generally the larger the indirect cost rate used.

To verify the reasonableness of the basis and calculations of indirect cost rates, management should compare grant money received to the actual indirect expenses. Depending on the difference, the organization may need to change the rate in the future.

As the process and calculations for indirect cost rates can be complicated and detailed, many government agencies provide specific guidance, such as the U.S. Department of Agriculture (USDA) that conducts webinars and provides other assistance, according to its website at http://nifa.usda.gov/business/indirect_cost_process.html.

Other government websites also disseminate information and provide examples of indirect cost rate process, format, and information required. You can check them out at:

http://www.epa.gov/ogd/recipient/sample1.htm

http://www.nsf.gov/bfa/dias/caar/docs/idcsubmissions.pdf

http://www.doi.gov/ibc/services/indirect_cost_services/FAQs.cfm

---

Grant Audit

As expected, the federal government is concerned that the grants provided are used properly, and consequently, requires audits of nonprofit recipients in addition to regular visits from the federal agency staff. Instead of having a separate audit of each major grant, the Single Audit allows for one independent audit covering all federal grant contracts.

These "Single Audits" and are required if the nonprofit has spent $750,000 or more in federal funds. (This threshold is likely to change in the future.) Single audits are performed by independent CPA firms, which usually carry out both regular and single audits within the same engagement, and release the results in two different reports—one for the regular portion and another for the grant audit.

When an auditor prepares the cost allocation plan or indirect cost proposal, he/she cannot do the grant audit if the indirect cost recovered is over $1 million.

During an audit, a CPA firm evaluates the fairness of the financial statements and the schedule of federal financial assistance, which contains information about grants. To this end, auditors evaluate risk by reviewing prior findings, internal controls, and usage of contractors. Additionally, CPA personnel should consider materiality of the funds, with major grants often getting most of the attention.

The Super Circular clarifies that auditors are responsible to follow up on any deficiencies, also called "findings." The nonprofit is supposed to respond with a corrective action plan. All of these documents are forwarded to the appropriate government agency.

Management should be aware of the cumulative grant spending, because as a nonprofit gets closer to the $750,000 in annual grant expenses, it should start budgeting for the single audit. It does not come cheap, and grant budgets may have to be adjusted to include this cost.

Other Grant Considerations

Federal grant contracts contain many details that warrant some attention since they may see odd to readers not familiar with grant compliance. Some issues to consider are:

Standard of Conduct

Nonprofits must implement written standards of conduct related to conflicts of interest and behavior of employees involved in the selection, award, and administration of grants. The government wants to avoid a situation where nonprofits utilize mostly businesses owned by board members, for example.

Computers

Computer devices under the nonprofit's capitalization policy or $5,000 are considered personal property at the same level as supplies. This decreases prior compliance requirements when computers were classified as equipment.

Royalties

The nonprofit may copyright federally funded work; however, the government reserves a royalty-free, nonexclusive, and irrevocable right to reproduce, publish, or otherwise use the work for federal purposes, including authorizing others to do so.

Bid

Fair competition and other requirements are required for federally funded purchases, except for micro purchases, which are typically $3,000 or less.

Sharing Information

The idea is for government agencies to share information and to analyze reports to improve programs and services across the board, spreading adoptions of practices that worked well for certain organizations.

Mandatory Disclosures

Nonprofits must disclose all violations of federal criminal law involving bribery, fraud, or gratuity violations that can potentially affect the federal award.

All the guidelines for proper government grants management are found in Office of Management and Budget circulars. They can be found online at http://www.whitehouse.gov/omb/circulars/index.htm

<u>**Summary**</u>

Nonprofits receiving government grants to fund programs and operations must follow the guidelines in the Super or Omni Circular, the federal government publication that unified old circulars. It specifies a standard 10 percent indirect cost rate and classifies computers and other equipment under $5,000 as supplies.

Organizations must recognize direct and indirect costs related to each grant program to be able to obtain a non-standard indirect cost rate after submitting a Cost Allocation Plan to the proper federal agency. The identification of the costs is also important to properly report and be reimbursed for both types of costs.

7

Financial Statements

"I know at last what distinguishes man from animals: financial worries."

Romain Rolland, French Writer, (1866-1944)

Nonprofits do not have owners per se, but they have many interested parties who are concerned about the organizations' financial well-being. Managers and boards of directors are attentive to fiscal matters in order to run the organization properly, while grantors may be more focused on financial issues involving grants.

Management and the board of directors typically get fiscal reports regularly that do not need to follow GAAP, but must be reliable to help managing organizations. These internal reports often compare actual numbers to budgets, helping managers identify problems and make good decisions.

While internal users like internal, budget reports, external users may prefer to receive GAAP-based financial statements because they are consistent and comparable to other nonprofits' reports. The GAAP statements must follow strict rules, making them the preferred format for many users, including bankers.

Users such as prospective and current donors might review financial statements, looking for signs of growth or problems. If a donor sees administrative expenses increasing while programs expenses are decreasing, it could raise some concerns. Maybe the organization is cutting down on programs. This trend may also be a sign that the organization is planning an expansion, hiring administrative personnel first; the situation may be temporary. To help users, notes and disclosures to the official financial statements provide more information on the numbers in the report.

This chapter covers reporting according to GAAP, as per FASB Document ASC-958, specific to nonprofits and other pronouncements. In the past, nonprofits followed SFAS 117, "Financial Statements of Not-for-Profit Organizations," but this report is now a part of FASB Accounting Standards Codification (ASC).

A nonprofit organization often releases fiscal reports that contain some similarities with for-profit company reporting. They are:

- **The Statement of Financial Position** – similar to the for-profit's Balance Sheet.

- **The Statement of Activities** – similar to the for-profit's Income Statement.

- **The Statement of Cash Flows** — similar to the for-profit's Cash Flow Statement (ASC 230 is specific to this report).

- **The Statement of Functional Expenses** — unique nonprofit report, showing details of expenses.

Statement of Financial Position

The Statement of Financial Position follows the formula:

Assets= Liabilities + Net Assets

This statement is similar to a for-profit company's balance sheet. The main difference is that instead of presenting "Retained Earnings," this statement shows "Net Assets."

The Statement of Financial Position typically presents information on all net assets, which can also be detailed in notes of financial statements. There are a few formats allowed by ASC 958-205 and 210, but we will be covering the most common and traditional presentation methods here.

As with the balance sheet, the focus of the Statement of Financial Position is to show the liquidity of an organization — it shows cash balances, accounts payable, and receivables. For instance, if a donor wants to donate $1 million to a charity, but sees $1,000 in cash, $2,000 in receivables, and over $100,000 in payables, this donor may wonder how the organization will pay this large liability and may not donate to the nonprofit.

The sequence of the items presented in this statement is based on liquidity, with the most liquid asset—cash—shown first, followed by current receivables. Liabilities are also shown based on those that are due first, followed by longer-term obligations. It's no surprise that banks often use the Statement of Financial Position to assess a nonprofit's liquidity and ability to pay back loans.

Nonprofits present the Statement of Financial Position in various ways, but the examples shown next—summary and classified versions— are the most popular styles. Showing two consecutive years is very common in nonprofit financial statements.

Summary version:

Do Good Organization
Statements of Financial Position
Dec. 31, 20X2 and 20X1

	20x2	20x1
Assets		
Cash and cash equivalents	xxx	xxx
Grant receivable-unrestricted	xxx	xxx
Prepaid expenses	xxx	xxx
Property and equipment	xxx	xxx
Assets restricted- perm.- Endowment	xxx	xxx
Total Assets	**xxx**	**xxx**
Liabilities		
Accounts payable	xxx	xxx
Deposits	xxx	xxx
Total Liabilities	**xxx**	**xxx**
Net Assets		
Unrestricted	xxx	xxx
Temporarily restricted	xxx	xxx
Permanently restricted	xxx	xxx
Total Net Assets	**xxx**	**xxx**
Total Liabilities and Net Assets	xxx	xxx

Classified statement version- one year only:

Do Good Organization
Statement of Financial Position
Dec. 31, 20X2

Assets	
Current Assets:	
Cash and cash equivalents	xxx
Short term investments	xxx
Grants receivable	xxx
Contributions receivable	
Unrestricted	xxx
Temporarily restricted	xxx
Total contribution receivable	xxx
Accounts receivable	xxx
Prepaid expenses	xxx
Total current assets	xxx
Property and equipment	xxx
Total Assets	xxx
Liabilities	
Current liabilities:	xxx
Accounts payable	xxx
Accrued expenses	xxx
Total current liabilities	xxx
Total liabilities	xxx
Net assets	
Unrestricted	xxx
Temporarily restricted	xxx
Permanently restricted	xxx
Total net assets	xxx
Total liabilities and net assets	xxx

Next are some interesting items on the Statement of Financial Position to be considered:

Cash and Cash Equivalents: This includes currency, petty cash, savings, and liquid, secure securities, such as U.S. Treasury bills.

Be careful with the cash balance number at year-end. I know of a too-aggressive accountant who moved funds from cash-bank accounts to investments, forgetting about outstanding checks. The result was an odd, negative cash balance at year-end.

Pledges or Grants Receivable: Commitments to donate shown at net realizable value—the amount the organization expects to receive. This number may be discounted and be net of an allowance for uncollectible pledges.

Prepaid Expenses: Amounts paid in advance that will become "real" expenses, as time passes. Usual examples are insurance payments and pre-paid rent.

Investments: Stocks, bonds, and other investments evaluated following GAAP accounting rules.

Fixed Assets or Property, Plant, and Equipment: This line reflects the net book value of fixed assets—original cost less accumulated depreciation.

Nonprofit organizations used to expense all fixed assets and not capitalize them. After 1994, nonprofits started to capitalize, as they were given the choice to do so. Therefore, many nonprofits may show odd numbers for assets on the books -- some capitalized and some not.

Accounts Payable: Amounts owed to vendors. Unpaid salaries, taxes, or other large liabilities may be reported separately.

Grants Payable: Promises made to individuals, businesses or other nonprofits.

Refundable Advances: These are also known as "Deposits" or "Deferred Revenue." They are amounts (not donations) received that belong to the future. For example, this might be a fee for a course scheduled in the following fiscal year.

Long-Term Debt: Principal and interest owed to creditors. The debt could be a bank loan, bond, or private debt financing.

Net Assets

Unrestricted Net assets; used for daily operations.

Temporarily restricted Net assets: revenues limited by donors' wishes. The money is allocated to a certain program or future date.

Permanently restricted Net assets: revenues limited by long-term donor-imposed stipulations. This net asset includes endowments.

There is some flexibility in the words used in the financial statements, where nonprofits can present "Donor Restricted Net Assets" or "Undesignated" net assets according to FASB ASC pronouncement Document 958, but the regular naming conventions of Unrestricted, Temporarily Restricted, and Permanently Restricted are preferred.

I have witnessed instances at nonprofits in which the board reviews only the Statement of Activities or a listing of income and expenses compared to budget amounts. Unfortunately, directors have no idea how much cash or receivables the nonprofit has in the bank, important information to have when making decisions. Boards should be sure to evaluate the Statement of Position, where the cash, receivables, and liabilities are listed.

Statement of Activities

The Statement of Activities follows the formula:

Revenues - Expenses = Change in Net Assets + Beginning Net Asset Balance = Ending Net Asset Balance

This report, the "Income Statement" of nonprofits, presents revenues and expenses during a certain period. However, instead of showing a net income or loss at the bottom, it shows a "change in net assets," "Increase in Net Assets" or a "Decrease in Net Assets." Then two lines follow, "Net assets at the Beginning of the Year" and "Net Assets at the End of the Year."

✓ **The term "Change in Net Assets" is equivalent to "Net Income or Loss" in the for-profit world.**

One of the major differences between the for-profit income statement and the nonprofit version is the net asset classification, often presented in columns, giving the Statement of Activities a matrix-like appearance. Columns are labeled according to each type of net asset, such as unrestricted, temporarily restricted, and permanently restricted.

Next is an example of the Statement of Activities showing the net assets in separate columns, a common presentation:

Do Very Good Organization
Statement of Activities
As of December 31, 20XX

	Unrestricted	Temporarily Restricted	Permanently Restricted	Total
REVENUES				
Contributions	3,050	1,000	5,000	9,050
Fundraising activities	500	300		800
Professional programs	100			100
Net assets released	300	(300)		
TOTAL REVENUES	3,950	1,000	5,000	9,950
EXPENSES				
Programs:				
Program A	350			350
Program B	220			220
Program C	150			150
Management and General	500			500
Fundraising	100			100
TOTAL EXPENSES	1,320			1,320
Change in net assets	2,630	1,000	5,000	8,630
Net Assets at beg. of year	2,500	500		3,000
Net Assets at end of year	5,130	1,500	5,000	11,630

Details of some items in this statement:

Contributions: Donations and contributions made by individuals or businesses, but not government grants (grants are presented separately).

Fundraising Activities: Revenues originated development activities, such as campaigns.

Professional Programs: Fees and other income received from programs.

Expenses: All expenses are shown as unrestricted, as expected. They are listed by program, management & general, and fundraising.

Net Assets Released from Restriction: Temporarily restricted revenue/net assets used during the current period. In this case, $300 was "moved" to the unrestricted net asset, resulting in a zero net effect overall.

Net Assets at the Beginning of the Year: Ending balance of the prior year brought forward.

Net Assets at the End of the Year: Beginning balance plus/minus changes in net assets. These numbers flow into the "Statement of Financial Position."

Expense details can be shown in this report, in the Statement of Functional Activities, or in the notes/disclosures often accompanying financial statements.

I have reviewed Statements of Position and tax returns that show nothing as fundraising, which is not usual. Most nonprofits typically present something under fundraising, such as postage or phone expenses. The absence of a number for fundraising raises the possibility of errors.

Statement of Cash Flows

The Statement of Cash Flows follows the formula:

Cash from Operations + Cash from Investing + Cash from Financing = Net increase/decrease in cash and cash equivalents + Beginning cash and cash equivalents = Cash and cash equivalents at the end of the year

This report is very similar to the for-profit cash flow statement. The report shows where cash came from and where it was used. This statement assists management, donors, and creditors in the following:

- Capacity to create positive cash flows in the future by analyzing history.

- Ability to pay program obligations and other fiscal obligations by analyzing cash flows.

- Evaluation of the differences between "Net assets increases/decreases" and cash receipts and payments.

- Assessment of details of cash and non-cash items, details of investments, and other fiscal transactions.

Per ASC 948-230, the Statement of Cash Flows is required as part of a nonprofit's financial statements set. It complements the other two financial reports, showing cash transactions not available on any other statement. As with the for-profit cash flow statement, this one shows cash flows in three categories:

Operating Activities: Includes all activities not related to investing or financing, such as receipts for general contributions. This section contains day-to-day cash activities, such as rent and supply payments along with unrestricted revenues.

Investing Activities: Includes cash flows related to purchases and sales of investments, such as plant and equipment.

Financing Activities: Includes the acquisition and repayment of capital, such as loans and payments. It also contains donations restricted for long-term purposes, such as cash received as an endowment.

The operating activities portion of this statement can be prepared using the direct or indirect method.

- ✓ The direct method specifies what the cash transactions were for, such as supplies or salaries.

- ✓ The indirect method shows increases and decreases in accounts, such as receivables or payable accounts.

The direct method is easier to understand and evaluate, while the indirect method is easier to compile, making it the preferred method for many organizations. FASB recommends the direct method, but still recognizes the indirect style. This may change in the future with the direct method being the only acceptable methodology.

A reconciliation between "net change (increase/decrease) in assets" to "net cash flow from operations" is required in both direct and indirect methods.

An example of a Cash Flow Statement using the indirect method:

Habitat House, Inc.
Statement of Cash Flows
Year Ended June 30, 20X7

CASH FLOWS FROM OPERATING ACTIVITIES		
Increase in net assets		200,000
Adjustments to reconcile Increase in net assets to net cash		
Depreciation		5,000
Increase in accounts payable		300
Increase in payroll tax liabilities		400
NET CASH PROVIDED BY OPERATING ACTIVITIES		**205,700**
CASH FLOWS FROM INVESTING ACTIVITIES		
Purchase of new Equipment		(5,000)
Short term investment-net		(1,000)
NET CASH FLOWS USED IN INVESTING ACTIVITIES		**(6,000)**
CASH FLOWS FROM FINANCING ACTIVITIES		
Capital Campaign		10,000
New men's shelter		2,000
Payments on loan		(500)
NET CASH PROVIDED BY FINANCING ACTIVITIES		11,500
NET INCREASE IN CASH AND CASH EQUIVALENTS		211,200
BEGINNING CASH AND CASH EQUIVALENTS		50,000
ENDING CASH AND CASH EQUIVALENTS		261,200

In this example, we see that depreciation was added back to the increase in net assets (net income in the for-profit world). This is because depreciation is not a cash transaction, but still decreases the net assets. Therefore, it should be added back to the net assets to get the proper cash flows.

Financing activities include restricted long-term money, such as funds from a Capital Campaign, as required by GAAP. Endowment payments would be presented under financing activities as well.

The increase in net assets should agree with the change in the Statement of Activities, while the ending cash and cash equivalents would agree with the cash balance in the Statement of Position.

One of the issues of the Statement of Cash Flows is the ability to compile the proper information. Even when created on a computer, this statement may contain errors.

As expected, banks are interested in this statement. If a nonprofit wants to increase its line of credit or obtain more loans, bank loan managers are likely to review this statement for clues about the risks of giving the organization more credit.

Statement of Functional Expenses

The Statement of Functional Expenses follows the formula:

Program Expenses + Administrative Expenses + Fundraising Expenses = Total Expenses

---

This statement is typical of nonprofit organizations and has no real counterpart in the for-profit world. The report helps users determine how effectively an organization is fulfilling its mission and using its resources. This statement can also be used to benchmark expenses and manage the nonprofit better.

Voluntary Health and Welfare organizations are required to show expense allocation information as a statement or as part of the footnotes. Other nonprofits are encouraged to show this information on the financial statements, but it is not required by GAAP.

✓ **The IRS requires a breakdown of functional expenses on Form 990, Part IX.**

The Statement of Functional Expenses is a matrix-like report, presenting headings for "Program Services" followed by "Supporting Services." Each of these headings usually involves a few columns. Program services header includes columns for each major program. Similarly, the supporting services header shows administrative and fundraising expenses, although it could also contain a column for membership development.

Additionally, the Statement of Functional Expenses shows natural categories, such as postage or rent as lines across the page. Each line is allocated among the functional columns. Thus, an expense, such as insurance, may have various numbers across, totaled on a last column.

Nonprofits use real, actual numbers in allocating expenses, not budget amounts. Often worksheets are used to compile this report. Accountants start with the total numbers from the accounting system and then go line by line, classifying each expense by functional area, based on backup supporting documentation.

Backups are likely to be time sheets, including electronic ones, invoices, etc. For example, nonprofits may allocate the utilities expense by using separate bills for each section, or they could allocate based on square footage of each area, assuming that is reasonable.

An example of a Statement of Functional Expenses follows.

Do-very-well-organization							
Statement of Functional Expenses							
6/30/20XX							
	ProgramServices				**Supporting Services**		
	Animal Advocacy	Public Education	Primate Sanctuary	Bird Program	Administration	Fundraising	Total
Personnel	546,999	112,333	98,746	18,746	155,236	58,999	$ 991,059
Consultants	62,333	57,949			19,972	27,881	$ 168,135
Legal and accounting	15,866		3,368	1,699	35,229		$ 56,162
Postage and delivery	10,496	99,687	235		10,103	12,587	$ 133,108
Print/publications	2,630	58,666			8,327	2,396	$ 72,019
Feed			128,991				$ 128,991
Depreciation	8,991	2,580	3,669	1,588	8,999	877	$ 26,704
Contributions	6,333						$ 6,333
Advertising/Promotion	47,777	26,888			2,041	11,982	$ 88,688
Investment expenses	10,001	8,613	7,863		5,284	3,954	$ 35,715
Travel and conferences	20,336	2,553	2,995	1,036	1,702	95	$ 28,717
Telecommunications	11,764	4,246	5,804		1,868	679	$ 24,361
Utilities	5,688	2,781	9,984		3,660	967	$ 23,080
Insurance	4,271	1,280	13,017		2,204	1,355	$ 22,127
Equipment	1,039	742	3,373		686	371	$ 6,211
Veterinary	8,941		2,445	778			$ 12,164
Maintenance			2,719				$ 2,719
Other	6,999	2,333	875		566	2,699	$ 13,472
Total	$ 770,464	$ 380,651	$ 284,084	$ 23,847	$ 255,877	$ 124,842	$1,839,765

The total lines should agree with the totals from the Statement of Activities. In this case for example, total administrative expenses of $255,877 must be on the Statement of Activities along with other totals for the expenses. The Statement of Activity may not show all details of programs, G&A and fundraising but the totals should tie in.

The program services section is spread into four columns because the organization has four major programs. In the example, expenses are up to par with expectations, with the programs area presenting the most expenses, followed by administration, and fundraising.

As is the case with many nonprofits, the salaries/personnel line shows the most expenses. Accordingly, organizations should pay attention to this area to make sure it is accurate and reasonable. Many times employees move around, working in different areas, but the payroll coding in the system remains the same, charging salaries to the wrong project or grant. Nonprofits' management should review changes to payroll coding (or lack of changes) and time sheets to make sure they are correct.

Some common problems with this functional statement are:

- Showing no fundraising expenses, but significant contribution revenue are presented in other reports

- Classifying all expenses as program expenses

- Changing the allocation significantly on the tax returns

Analysis of Financial Statements

Management and donors often analyze financial statements to make informed decisions and identify trends. Each statement gives a different perspective on the fiscal health of an organization, such as how much cash is in the bank and the amount and type of expenses. However, it is important to analyze each number as it relates to the others, to identify fiscal strengths and weaknesses of an organization.

Budget Analysis

Reviewing actual numbers versus budget is the first and most common way of analyzing financial statements. Managers review the numbers to see if any intervention is required. For example, if contributions revenue is significantly below budget, fundraising may need to be ramped up or costs may need to be reduced.

When conducting this analysis, it is important to review monthly and year-to-day variances to evaluate the cumulative impact of the differences. The board at a nonprofit I worked at only looked at monthly and quarterly "Actual vs. Budget" reports, missing the mounting effect of smaller variances. It ended the year having to use its reserve funds to pay the bills. Had the board evaluated cumulative differences, it may have increased fundraising earlier to avoid having to use reserves.

Review Past Financial Statements

A good way to evaluate financial statements is to look at past reports, so that any significant changes can be identified and evaluated. As many reports include numbers for two years, this comparison can be done easily, but older statements should also be considered to get a better view of the economic situation of the nonprofit.

For example, if liabilities have doubled from one year to the next, the organization may be facing fiscal troubles, or there may be a strategic reason for the increase in liabilities, maybe related to an expansion of programs. Reviewing past information is a good way to start analyzing the fiscal numbers to see how the nonprofit is performing and how the money is used.

Review Statements of Other Organizations

Financial statements from other organizations can be picked up from their websites, or from Guidestar.com, which presents tax returns containing financial statement information. Be sure to review information from similar nonprofits in terms of size and niche. A small social work organization could be compared to other small nonprofits for the analysis to be useful.

Publications geared towards nonprofits, such as "Nonprofits Times" or the "Journal of Philanthropy" often conduct research and publish fiscal information that are used by the organization as benchmarks.

Focus on a Few Numbers

Looking at just one item, such as cash, does not give you enough information. However, if you see $100 as the cash balance, $200 in current receivables, and $8,000 in current liabilities, you are likely to be concerned about how the organization will pay its bills and be in business for long.

You may also compare the revenues section on the Statement of Activities with the cash and receivables on the Statement of Position. The revenues may be $20,000, but if you see $18,000 in receivables and $100 in cash, it is likely that most of the revenues consist of uncollected pledges, putting the organization at risk for poor cash flows.

Use Ratios

Ratios, quick ways to assess relationships between the financial numbers, are used to analyze both nonprofit and for-profit organizations. By using ratios, one can compare fiscal data without reviewing the details, making comparisons among several organizations easier tasks. Instead of reviewing cash balances of two organizations, users may look at current ratios, for instance, giving them additional information.

Users may pick up the numbers from organizations' websites and tax returns, available at www.guidestar.com. Next are some useful ratios:

Name of Ratio	Formula	Goal
Current Ratio	Current Assets/Current Liabilities	Measure the ability of an organization to pay its current debt
Debt Ratio	Total Liabilities/Total Unrestricted Net Assets	Assess unrestricted funds' ability to pay bills, loans, and the existence of any "cushion" leftover
Administration Cost Ratio	Total Fundraising+General and Admin. Expense/Total Expenses	Common ratio used to assess how certain expenses are allocated
Fundraising Efficiency	Contributed Income/Fundraising Expenses	Average amount of contributions raised from a dollar spent on fundraising

<u>Summary</u>

Nonprofits release common financial statements, such as the Statement of Position, Statement of Activities, and Statement of Cash Flows. Additionally, many nonprofits need to prepare the Statement of Functional Expenses, showing costs in a matrix-like format or as part of footnotes.

Analysis of these financial statements can provide information about the ability of a nonprofit to pay its bills, grow, and remain in business. A common analysis is to use the actual vs. budgets reports as an analysis mechanism, but other tools, such as ratios and reviews of fiscal reports of similar organizations could also be employed.

Sheila Shanker

8

Taxation

"The hardest thing to understand in the world is the income tax."

Albert Einstein

It can be a surprise to know that nonprofit organizations file tax returns, even though they are tax-exempt. Many times, organizations file information returns, but at other times, federal, state, or local taxes are also paid. This chapter focuses on the federal reporting requirements.

The IRS, the main U.S. tax agency, provides guidelines for nonprofit tax returns, which can be quite detailed, including numbers and descriptions of mission statements, programs, and other pertinent information. The IRS website, www.irs.gov, offers both the tax forms and instructions for current and past years that can be downloaded or printed out.

Note that the tax returns for nonprofits have changed significantly since 2008. Before, the IRS required less information overall about the organization. The earlier version had less schedules and no questions related to internal controls and other issues, as it is now the case.

Usually, nonprofits must file one or more of these tax returns annually, by the 15th day of the fifth month after the closing of the year:

- 990: *Return of Organization Exempt from Income Tax-* Regular tax return for nonprofits
- 990-EZ: *Short Form Return of Organization Exempt from Income Tax-* Summarized version of the tax return for smaller organizations
- 990-N*: e-Postcard-* Basic information for small nonprofits
- 990-T: *Exempt Organization Business Income Tax Return -* For taxable transactions incurred

Of all the tax forms, the 990-N is the newest, available for filing online only at http://epostcard.form990.org. This online filing requests basic information about an organization, such as name, federal ID, and address.

✓ **Extensions of time to file returns are available.**

With all these options, what form should a nonprofit use? Organizations decide which form to fill out based on the IRS guidelines posted at the IRS website or published guidelines. The gross receipts and assets amounts are likely to change every year, so accountants must review the IRS rules each year to be sure they are ready to file the correct tax return.

The IRS offers fill-in tax forms on its website that can be downloaded and saved. However, the forms do not allow for calculations, which must be figured manually, often decreasing accuracy. The filing requirements from the IRS website are shown below. As the threshold for filing changes often, be sure to check the IRS website before filing.

For year 2014

Gross receipts normally ≤ $50,000 Note: Organizations eligible to file the *e-Postcard* may choose to file a full return	990-N
Gross receipts < $200,000, and Total assets < $500,000	990-EZ or 990
Gross receipts ≥ $200,000, or Total assets ≥ $500,000	990

Nonprofits with receipts "normally" below or above a certain amount, as mentioned in the schedule, refers to the average of all receipts from three consecutive years, including the current year. For example, a nonprofit has gross receipts of $60,000 in 2014, $55,000 in 2013, and $30,000 in 2012. The average is $48,333, and the organization can file Form 990-N in 2014.

The 990 is quite comprehensive, involving fiscal and other data, such as the mission statement, description of programs, number of volunteers, and disclosure of certain policies and procedures. The IRS wants to have an overall idea about the organization, not just fiscal data.

The IRS requires nonprofits to fill out the core pages of the 990 or 990-EZ and any other schedule. Form 990-Part IV is a checklist for nonprofits to identify such required schedules. Another section of the 990, Part VI, specifically relates to governance, management, and disclosures. It asks questions hinting at internal controls nonprofits should have, such as Item 13: "Did the organization have a whistleblower policy?"

✓ **If organizations do not file taxes for three consecutive years, the IRS revokes their tax-exempt status- even small 990-N filers.**

Nonprofits should be concerned with losing their tax-exempt classification because this can create many problems. For example, donors will not be able to deduct their donations on their tax returns and that may be unpleasant. Additionally, many grant applications are available online and will be rejected right away if the Employer ID Number does not match the IRS master list of tax-exempt organizations.

The IRS has established fines for large organizations that file 990 or 990-EZ late. "If an organization whose gross receipts are less than $1,000,000 for its tax year files its Form 990 after the due date (including any extensions), and the organization does not provide reasonable cause for filing late, the Internal Revenue Service will impose a penalty of $20 per day for each day the return is late. The maximum penalty is $10,000, or 5 percent of the organization's gross receipts, whichever is less. The penalty increases to $100 per day, up to a maximum of $50,000, for an organization whose gross receipts exceed $1,000,000" (www.irs.gov).

To show "reasonable cause" the organization should include information indicating that the organization was not neglectful or careless, but that it had good reasons for not filing for an extension (if applicable). In addition, the organization must specify the steps it will take to avoid filing late again. A history of late filing does not bode well for the nonprofit. Forgetting to file is not good enough, although ignorance of the filing requirements by a 100 percent volunteer organization may be a reasonable cause.

Once a nonprofit fails to file on time, the IRS sends out a letter with a date for the return to be filed. If the returns are not filed by that day, the person responsible is charged $10 a day, up to a maximum of $5,000. If more than one person is responsible for filing, the penalties are shared between them.

Form 990

This form is usually filled out by the nonprofit's accounting manager or by outside auditors, as part of the audit engagement. One of the ideas behind the form is to make the board of directors more involved and responsible regarding the tax returns. To illustrate, Part VI-Section B-Policies, line 11a asks, "Has the organization provided a complete copy of this Form 990 to all members of its governing body before filing the form?" Line 11b requires the organization to describe the process of reviewing Form 990 in Schedule O.

Forms 990 and 990EZ are detailed, including a core and schedules to be used on an as-needed basis. Since the forms and schedules are public documents reviewed by the IRS, nonprofits and auditors should be very careful in preparing them. The core 990 pages are presented with some explanations following.

Form **990**	**Return of Organization Exempt From Income Tax**	OMB No. 1545-0047
	Under section 501(c), 527, or 4947(a)(1) of the Internal Revenue Code (except private foundations)	**2014**
Department of the Treasury Internal Revenue Service	▶ Do not enter social security numbers on this form as it may be made public. ▶ Information about Form 990 and its instructions is at www.irs.gov/form990.	**Open to Public Inspection**

A For the 2014 calendar year, or tax year beginning _____ , 2014, and ending _____ , 20 __

B Check if applicable:	**C** Name of organization			**D** Employer identification number
☐ Address change	Doing business as			
☐ Name change	Number and street (or P.O. box if mail is not delivered to street address)	Room/suite		**E** Telephone number
☐ Initial return				
☐ Final return/terminated	City or town, state or province, country, and ZIP or foreign postal code			
☐ Amended return				**G** Gross receipts $
☐ Application pending	**F** Name and address of principal officer:		H(a) Is this a group return for subordinates? ☐ Yes ☐ No
			H(b) Are all subordinates included? ☐ Yes ☐ No
			If "No," attach a list. (see instructions)
I Tax-exempt status: ☐ 501(c)(3) ☐ 501(c) ( ) ◀ (insert no.) ☐ 4947(a)(1) or ☐ 527			
J Website: ▶			H(c) Group exemption number ▶
K Form of organization: ☐ Corporation ☐ Trust ☐ Association ☐ Other ▶	**L** Year of formation:	**M** State of legal domicile:

Part I Summary

1	Briefly describe the organization's mission or most significant activities:		
2	Check this box ▶ ☐ if the organization discontinued its operations or disposed of more than 25% of its net assets.		
3	Number of voting members of the governing body (Part VI, line 1a)	**3**	
4	Number of independent voting members of the governing body (Part VI, line 1b)	**4**	
5	Total number of individuals employed in calendar year 2014 (Part V, line 2a)	**5**	
6	Total number of volunteers (estimate if necessary)	**6**	
7a	Total unrelated business revenue from Part VIII, column (C), line 12	**7a**	
b	Net unrelated business taxable income from Form 990-T, line 34	**7b**	

		Prior Year	Current Year
8	Contributions and grants (Part VIII, line 1h)		
9	Program service revenue (Part VIII, line 2g)		
10	Investment income (Part VIII, column (A), lines 3, 4, and 7d)		
11	Other revenue (Part VIII, column (A), lines 5, 6d, 8c, 9c, 10c, and 11e) . . .		
12	Total revenue—add lines 8 through 11 (must equal Part VIII, column (A), line 12)		
13	Grants and similar amounts paid (Part IX, column (A), lines 1–3)		
14	Benefits paid to or for members (Part IX, column (A), line 4)		
15	Salaries, other compensation, employee benefits (Part IX, column (A), lines 5–10)		
16a	Professional fundraising fees (Part IX, column (A), line 11e)		
b	Total fundraising expenses (Part IX, column (D), line 25) ▶ _____		
17	Other expenses (Part IX, column (A), lines 11a–11d, 11f–24e)		
18	Total expenses. Add lines 13–17 (must equal Part IX, column (A), line 25) .		
19	Revenue less expenses. Subtract line 18 from line 12		

		Beginning of Current Year	End of Year
20	Total assets (Part X, line 16)		
21	Total liabilities (Part X, line 26)		
22	Net assets or fund balances. Subtract line 21 from line 20		

Part II Signature Block

Under penalties of perjury, I declare that I have examined this return, including accompanying schedules and statements, and to the best of my knowledge and belief, it is true, correct, and complete. Declaration of preparer (other than officer) is based on all information of which preparer has any knowledge.

Sign Here	Signature of officer			Date	
	Type or print name and title				

Paid Preparer Use Only	Print/Type preparer's name	Preparer's signature	Date	Check ☐ if self-employed	PTIN
	Firm's name ▶			Firm's EIN ▶	
	Firm's address ▶			Phone no.	

May the IRS discuss this return with the preparer shown above? (see instructions) . . . . ☐ Yes ☐ No

For Paperwork Reduction Act Notice, see the separate instructions.   Cat. No. 11282Y   Form **990** (2014)

Form 990 (2014)   Page **2**

Part III Statement of Program Service Accomplishments

Check if Schedule O contains a response or note to any line in this Part III . . . . ☐

1 Briefly describe the organization's mission:

_____

_____

_____

_____

2 Did the organization undertake any significant program services during the year which were not listed on the
prior Form 990 or 990-EZ? . . . . ☐ Yes ☐ No

If "Yes," describe these new services on Schedule O.

3 Did the organization cease conducting, or make significant changes in how it conducts, any program
services? . . . . ☐ Yes ☐ No

If "Yes," describe these changes on Schedule O.

4 Describe the organization's program service accomplishments for each of its three largest program services, as measured by
expenses. Section 501(c)(3) and 501(c)(4) organizations are required to report the amount of grants and allocations to others,
the total expenses, and revenue, if any, for each program service reported.

4a (Code: _____) (Expenses $ _____ including grants of $ _____) (Revenue $ _____)

_____

_____

_____

_____

_____

_____

_____

_____

_____

4b (Code: _____) (Expenses $ _____ including grants of $ _____) (Revenue $ _____)

_____

_____

_____

_____

_____

_____

_____

_____

_____

4c (Code: _____) (Expenses $ _____ including grants of $ _____) (Revenue $ _____)

_____

_____

_____

_____

_____

_____

_____

_____

_____

4d Other program services (Describe in Schedule O.)

(Expenses $ _____ including grants of $ _____) (Revenue $ _____)

4e Total program service expenses ▶ _____

Form **990** (2014)

Part IV **Checklist of Required Schedules**

		Yes	No
1	Is the organization described in section 501(c)(3) or 4947(a)(1) (other than a private foundation)? If "Yes," complete Schedule A **1**		
2	Is the organization required to complete Schedule B, Schedule of Contributors (see instructions)? . . . **2**		
3	Did the organization engage in direct or indirect political campaign activities on behalf of or in opposition to candidates for public office? If "Yes," complete Schedule C, Part I **3**		
4	**Section 501(c)(3) organizations.** Did the organization engage in lobbying activities, or have a section 501(h) election in effect during the tax year? If "Yes," complete Schedule C, Part II **4**		
5	Is the organization a section 501(c)(4), 501(c)(5), or 501(c)(6) organization that receives membership dues, assessments, or similar amounts as defined in Revenue Procedure 98-19? If "Yes," complete Schedule C, Part III **5**		
6	Did the organization maintain any donor advised funds or any similar funds or accounts for which donors have the right to provide advice on the distribution or investment of amounts in such funds or accounts? If "Yes," complete Schedule D, Part I **6**		
7	Did the organization receive or hold a conservation easement, including easements to preserve open space, the environment, historic land areas, or historic structures? If "Yes," complete Schedule D, Part II . . . **7**		
8	Did the organization maintain collections of works of art, historical treasures, or other similar assets? If "Yes," complete Schedule D, Part III **8**		
9	Did the organization report an amount in Part X, line 21, for escrow or custodial account liability; serve as a custodian for amounts not listed in Part X; or provide credit counseling, debt management, credit repair, or debt negotiation services? If "Yes," complete Schedule D, Part IV **9**		
10	Did the organization, directly or through a related organization, hold assets in temporarily restricted endowments, permanent endowments, or quasi-endowments? If "Yes," complete Schedule D, Part V . . **10**		
11	If the organization's answer to any of the following questions is "Yes," then complete Schedule D, Parts VI, VII, VIII, IX, or X as applicable.		
a	Did the organization report an amount for land, buildings, and equipment in Part X, line 10? If "Yes," complete Schedule D, Part VI **11a**		
b	Did the organization report an amount for investments—other securities in Part X, line 12 that is 5% or more of its total assets reported in Part X, line 16? If "Yes," complete Schedule D, Part VII **11b**		
c	Did the organization report an amount for investments—program related in Part X, line 13 that is 5% or more of its total assets reported in Part X, line 16? If "Yes," complete Schedule D, Part VIII **11c**		
d	Did the organization report an amount for other assets in Part X, line 15 that is 5% or more of its total assets reported in Part X, line 16? If "Yes," complete Schedule D, Part IX **11d**		
e	Did the organization report an amount for other liabilities in Part X, line 25? If "Yes," complete Schedule D, Part X **11e**		
f	Did the organization's separate or consolidated financial statements for the tax year include a footnote that addresses the organization's liability for uncertain tax positions under FIN 48 (ASC 740)? If "Yes," complete Schedule D, Part X . . **11f**		
12 a	Did the organization obtain separate, independent audited financial statements for the tax year? If "Yes," complete Schedule D, Parts XI and XII **12a**		
b	Was the organization included in consolidated, independent audited financial statements for the tax year? If "Yes," and if the organization answered "No" to line 12a, then completing Schedule D, Parts XI and XII is optional **12b**		
13	Is the organization a school described in section 170(b)(1)(A)(ii)? If "Yes," complete Schedule E . . . **13**		
14 a	Did the organization maintain an office, employees, or agents outside of the United States? **14a**		
b	Did the organization have aggregate revenues or expenses of more than $10,000 from grantmaking, fundraising, business, investment, and program service activities outside the United States, or aggregate foreign investments valued at $100,000 or more? If "Yes," complete Schedule F, Parts I and IV. **14b**		
15	Did the organization report on Part IX, column (A), line 3, more than $5,000 of grants or other assistance to or for any foreign organization? If "Yes," complete Schedule F, Parts II and IV **15**		
16	Did the organization report on Part IX, column (A), line 3, more than $5,000 of aggregate grants or other assistance to or for foreign individuals? If "Yes," complete Schedule F, Parts III and IV. **16**		
17	Did the organization report a total of more than $15,000 of expenses for professional fundraising services on Part IX, column (A), lines 6 and 11e? If "Yes," complete Schedule G, Part I (see instructions) **17**		
18	Did the organization report more than $15,000 total of fundraising event gross income and contributions on Part VIII, lines 1c and 8a? If "Yes," complete Schedule G, Part II **18**		
19	Did the organization report more than $15,000 of gross income from gaming activities on Part VIII, line 9a? If "Yes," complete Schedule G, Part III **19**		
20 a	Did the organization operate one or more hospital facilities? If "Yes," complete Schedule H **20a**		
b	If "Yes" to line 20a, did the organization attach a copy of its audited financial statements to this return? . **20b**		

Nonprofit Finance: A Practical Guide

Part IV	Checklist of Required Schedules *(continued)*			
			Yes	No
21	Did the organization report more than $5,000 of grants or other assistance to any domestic organization or domestic government on Part IX, column (A), line 1? *If "Yes," complete Schedule I, Parts I and II*	**21**		
22	Did the organization report more than $5,000 of grants or other assistance to or for domestic individuals on Part IX, column (A), line 2? *If "Yes," complete Schedule I, Parts I and III*	**22**		
23	Did the organization answer "Yes" to Part VII, Section A, line 3, 4, or 5 about compensation of the organization's current and former officers, directors, trustees, key employees, and highest compensated employees? *If "Yes," complete Schedule J*	**23**		
24a	Did the organization have a tax-exempt bond issue with an outstanding principal amount of more than $100,000 as of the last day of the year, that was issued after December 31, 2002? *If "Yes," answer lines 24b through 24d and complete Schedule K. If "No," go to line 25a*	**24a**		
b	Did the organization invest any proceeds of tax-exempt bonds beyond a temporary period exception? . .	**24b**		
c	Did the organization maintain an escrow account other than a refunding escrow at any time during the year to defease any tax-exempt bonds?	**24c**		
d	Did the organization act as an "on behalf of" issuer for bonds outstanding at any time during the year? . .	**24d**		
25a	**Section 501(c)(3), 501(c)(4), and 501(c)(29) organizations.** Did the organization engage in an excess benefit transaction with a disqualified person during the year? *If "Yes," complete Schedule L, Part I*	**25a**		
b	Is the organization aware that it engaged in an excess benefit transaction with a disqualified person in a prior year, and that the transaction has not been reported on any of the organization's prior Forms 990 or 990-EZ? *If "Yes," complete Schedule L, Part I*	**25b**		
26	Did the organization report any amount on Part X, line 5, 6, or 22 for receivables from or payables to any current or former officers, directors, trustees, key employees, highest compensated employees, or disqualified persons? *If "Yes," complete Schedule L, Part II*	**26**		
27	Did the organization provide a grant or other assistance to an officer, director, trustee, key employee, substantial contributor or employee thereof, a grant selection committee member, or to a 35% controlled entity or family member of any of these persons? *If "Yes," complete Schedule L, Part III*	**27**		
28	Was the organization a party to a business transaction with one of the following parties (see Schedule L, Part IV instructions for applicable filing thresholds, conditions, and exceptions):			
a	A current or former officer, director, trustee, or key employee? *If "Yes," complete Schedule L, Part IV* . .	**28a**		
b	A family member of a current or former officer, director, trustee, or key employee? *If "Yes," complete Schedule L, Part IV*	**28b**		
c	An entity of which a current or former officer, director, trustee, or key employee (or a family member thereof) was an officer, director, trustee, or direct or indirect owner? *If "Yes," complete Schedule L, Part IV* . .	**28c**		
29	Did the organization receive more than $25,000 in non-cash contributions? *If "Yes," complete Schedule M*	**29**		
30	Did the organization receive contributions of art, historical treasures, or other similar assets, or qualified conservation contributions? *If "Yes," complete Schedule M*	**30**		
31	Did the organization liquidate, terminate, or dissolve and cease operations? *If "Yes," complete Schedule N, Part I*	**31**		
32	Did the organization sell, exchange, dispose of, or transfer more than 25% of its net assets? *If "Yes," complete Schedule N, Part II*	**32**		
33	Did the organization own 100% of an entity disregarded as separate from the organization under Regulations sections 301.7701-2 and 301.7701-3? *If "Yes," complete Schedule R, Part I*	**33**		
34	Was the organization related to any tax-exempt or taxable entity? *If "Yes," complete Schedule R, Part II, III, or IV, and Part V, line 1*	**34**		
35a	Did the organization have a controlled entity within the meaning of section 512(b)(13)?	**35a**		
b	If "Yes" to line 35a, did the organization receive any payment from or engage in any transaction with a controlled entity within the meaning of section 512(b)(13)? *If "Yes," complete Schedule R, Part V, line 2* . .	**35b**		
36	**Section 501(c)(3) organizations.** Did the organization make any transfers to an exempt non-charitable related organization? *If "Yes," complete Schedule R, Part V, line 2*	**36**		
37	Did the organization conduct more than 5% of its activities through an entity that is not a related organization and that is treated as a partnership for federal income tax purposes? *If "Yes," complete Schedule R, Part VI*	**37**		
38	Did the organization complete Schedule O and provide explanations in Schedule O for Part VI, lines 11b and 19? **Note.** All Form 990 filers are required to complete Schedule O	**38**		

Sheila Shanker

Form 990 (2014) Page **5**

Part V Statements Regarding Other IRS Filings and Tax Compliance

Check if Schedule O contains a response or note to any line in this Part V . . . . ☐

			Yes	No
1a	Enter the number reported in Box 3 of Form 1096. Enter -0- if not applicable	1a		
b	Enter the number of Forms W-2G included in line 1a. Enter -0- if not applicable	1b		
c	Did the organization comply with backup withholding rules for reportable payments to vendors and reportable gaming (gambling) winnings to prize winners?	1c		
2a	Enter the number of employees reported on Form W-3, Transmittal of Wage and Tax Statements, filed for the calendar year ending with or within the year covered by this return	2a		
b	If at least one is reported on line 2a, did the organization file all required federal employment tax returns? .	2b		
	Note. If the sum of lines 1a and 2a is greater than 250, you may be required to e-file (see instructions) . .			
3a	Did the organization have unrelated business gross income of $1,000 or more during the year?	3a		
b	If "Yes," has it filed a Form 990-T for this year? If "No" to line 3b, provide an explanation in Schedule O . .	3b		
4a	At any time during the calendar year, did the organization have an interest in, or a signature or other authority over, a financial account in a foreign country (such as a bank account, securities account, or other financial account)?	4a		
b	If "Yes," enter the name of the foreign country: ▶			
	See instructions for filing requirements for FinCEN Form 114, Report of Foreign Bank and Financial Accounts (FBAR).			
5a	Was the organization a party to a prohibited tax shelter transaction at any time during the tax year? . . .	5a		
b	Did any taxable party notify the organization that it was or is a party to a prohibited tax shelter transaction?	5b		
c	If "Yes" to line 5a or 5b, did the organization file Form 8886-T?	5c		
6a	Does the organization have annual gross receipts that are normally greater than $100,000, and did the organization solicit any contributions that were not tax deductible as charitable contributions?	6a		
b	If "Yes," did the organization include with every solicitation an express statement that such contributions or gifts were not tax deductible?	6b		
7	**Organizations that may receive deductible contributions under section 170(c).**			
a	Did the organization receive a payment in excess of $75 made partly as a contribution and partly for goods and services provided to the payor?	7a		
b	If "Yes," did the organization notify the donor of the value of the goods or services provided?	7b		
c	Did the organization sell, exchange, or otherwise dispose of tangible personal property for which it was required to file Form 8282?	7c		
d	If "Yes," indicate the number of Forms 8282 filed during the year	7d		
e	Did the organization receive any funds, directly or indirectly, to pay premiums on a personal benefit contract?	7e		
f	Did the organization, during the year, pay premiums, directly or indirectly, on a personal benefit contract? .	7f		
g	If the organization received a contribution of qualified intellectual property, did the organization file Form 8899 as required?	7g		
h	If the organization received a contribution of cars, boats, airplanes, or other vehicles, did the organization file a Form 1098-C?	7h		
8	**Sponsoring organizations maintaining donor advised funds.** Did a donor advised fund maintained by the sponsoring organization have excess business holdings at any time during the year?	8		
9	**Sponsoring organizations maintaining donor advised funds.**			
a	Did the sponsoring organization make any taxable distributions under section 4966?	9a		
b	Did the sponsoring organization make a distribution to a donor, donor advisor, or related person? . . .	9b		
10	**Section 501(c)(7) organizations.** Enter:			
a	Initiation fees and capital contributions included on Part VIII, line 12	10a		
b	Gross receipts, included on Form 990, Part VIII, line 12, for public use of club facilities .	10b		
11	**Section 501(c)(12) organizations.** Enter:			
a	Gross income from members or shareholders	11a		
b	Gross income from other sources (Do not net amounts due or paid to other sources against amounts due or received from them.)	11b		
12a	**Section 4947(a)(1) non-exempt charitable trusts.** Is the organization filing Form 990 in lieu of Form 1041?	12a		
b	If "Yes," enter the amount of tax-exempt interest received or accrued during the year . .	12b		
13	**Section 501(c)(29) qualified nonprofit health insurance issuers.**			
a	Is the organization licensed to issue qualified health plans in more than one state?	13a		
	Note. See the instructions for additional information the organization must report on Schedule O.			
b	Enter the amount of reserves the organization is required to maintain by the states in which the organization is licensed to issue qualified health plans	13b		
c	Enter the amount of reserves on hand	13c		
14a	Did the organization receive any payments for indoor tanning services during the tax year?	14a		
b	If "Yes," has it filed a Form 720 to report these payments? If "No," provide an explanation in Schedule O .	14b		

Form **990** (2014)

146

Form 990 (2014)   Page **6**

Part VI   **Governance, Management, and Disclosure** *For each "Yes" response to lines 2 through 7b below, and for a "No" response to line 8a, 8b, or 10b below, describe the circumstances, processes, or changes in Schedule O. See instructions.*

Check if Schedule O contains a response or note to any line in this Part VI . . . . ☐

Section A. Governing Body and Management

			Yes	No
1a	Enter the number of voting members of the governing body at the end of the tax year . .	1a		
	If there are material differences in voting rights among members of the governing body, or if the governing body delegated broad authority to an executive committee or similar committee, explain in Schedule O.			
b	Enter the number of voting members included in line 1a, above, who are independent . .	1b		
2	Did any officer, director, trustee, or key employee have a family relationship or a business relationship with any other officer, director, trustee, or key employee?	2		
3	Did the organization delegate control over management duties customarily performed by or under the direct supervision of officers, directors, or trustees, or key employees to a management company or other person? .	3		
4	Did the organization make any significant changes to its governing documents since the prior Form 990 was filed?	4		
5	Did the organization become aware during the year of a significant diversion of the organization's assets? .	5		
6	Did the organization have members or stockholders?	6		
7a	Did the organization have members, stockholders, or other persons who had the power to elect or appoint one or more members of the governing body?	7a		
b	Are any governance decisions of the organization reserved to (or subject to approval by) members, stockholders, or persons other than the governing body?	7b		
8	Did the organization contemporaneously document the meetings held or written actions undertaken during the year by the following:			
a	The governing body?	8a		
b	Each committee with authority to act on behalf of the governing body?	8b		
9	Is there any officer, director, trustee, or key employee listed in Part VII, Section A, who cannot be reached at the organization's mailing address? *If "Yes," provide the names and addresses in Schedule O*	9		

Section B. Policies *(This Section B requests information about policies not required by the Internal Revenue Code.)*

			Yes	No
10a	Did the organization have local chapters, branches, or affiliates?	10a		
b	If "Yes," did the organization have written policies and procedures governing the activities of such chapters, affiliates, and branches to ensure their operations are consistent with the organization's exempt purposes?	10b		
11a	Has the organization provided a complete copy of this Form 990 to all members of its governing body before filing the form?	11a		
b	Describe in Schedule O the process, if any, used by the organization to review this Form 990.			
12a	Did the organization have a written conflict of interest policy? *If "No," go to line 13*	12a		
b	Were officers, directors, or trustees, and key employees required to disclose annually interests that could give rise to conflicts?	12b		
c	Did the organization regularly and consistently monitor and enforce compliance with the policy? *If "Yes," describe in Schedule O how this was done*	12c		
13	Did the organization have a written whistleblower policy?	13		
14	Did the organization have a written document retention and destruction policy?	14		
15	Did the process for determining compensation of the following persons include a review and approval by independent persons, comparability data, and contemporaneous substantiation of the deliberation and decision?			
a	The organization's CEO, Executive Director, or top management official	15a		
b	Other officers or key employees of the organization	15b		
	If "Yes" to line 15a or 15b, describe the process in Schedule O (see instructions).			
16a	Did the organization invest in, contribute assets to, or participate in a joint venture or similar arrangement with a taxable entity during the year?	16a		
b	If "Yes," did the organization follow a written policy or procedure requiring the organization to evaluate its participation in joint venture arrangements under applicable federal tax law, and take steps to safeguard the organization's exempt status with respect to such arrangements?	16b		

Section C. Disclosure

17   List the states with which a copy of this Form 990 is required to be filed ▶

18   Section 6104 requires an organization to make its Forms 1023 (or 1024 if applicable), 990, and 990-T (Section 501(c)(3)s only) available for public inspection. Indicate how you made these available. Check all that apply.

     ☐ Own website   ☐ Another's website   ☐ Upon request   ☐ Other *(explain in Schedule O)*

19   Describe in Schedule O whether (and if so, how) the organization made its governing documents, conflict of interest policy, and financial statements available to the public during the tax year.

20   State the name, address, and telephone number of the person who possesses the organization's books and records: ▶

Form **990** (2014)

147

Form 990 (2014)   Page **7**

Part VII Compensation of Officers, Directors, Trustees, Key Employees, Highest Compensated Employees, and Independent Contractors

Check if Schedule O contains a response or note to any line in this Part VII . . . . ☐

Section A. Officers, Directors, Trustees, Key Employees, and Highest Compensated Employees

1a Complete this table for all persons required to be listed. Report compensation for the calendar year ending with or within the organization's tax year.

• List all of the organization's **current** officers, directors, trustees (whether individuals or organizations), regardless of amount of compensation. Enter -0- in columns (D), (E), and (F) if no compensation was paid.

• List all of the organization's **current** key employees, if any. See instructions for definition of "key employee."

• List the organization's five **current** highest compensated employees (other than an officer, director, trustee, or key employee) who received reportable compensation (Box 5 of Form W-2 and/or Box 7 of Form 1099-MISC) of more than $100,000 from the organization and any related organizations.

• List all of the organization's **former** officers, key employees, and highest compensated employees who received more than $100,000 of reportable compensation from the organization and any related organizations.

• List all of the organization's **former directors or trustees** that received, in the capacity as a former director or trustee of the organization, more than $10,000 of reportable compensation from the organization and any related organizations.

List persons in the following order: individual trustees or directors; institutional trustees; officers; key employees; highest compensated employees; and former such persons.

☐ Check this box if neither the organization nor any related organization compensated any current officer, director, or trustee.

(A) Name and Title	(B) Average hours per week (list any hours for related organizations below dotted line)	(C) Position (do not check more than one box, unless person is both an officer and a director/trustee)						(D) Reportable compensation from the organization (W-2/1099-MISC)	(E) Reportable compensation from related organizations (W-2/1099-MISC)	(F) Estimated amount of other compensation from the organization and related organizations
		Individual trustee or director	Institutional trustee	Officer	Key employee	Highest compensated employee	Former			
(1)										
(2)										
(3)										
(4)										
(5)										
(6)										
(7)										
(8)										
(9)										
(10)										
(11)										
(12)										
(13)										
(14)										

Form **990** (2014)

Part VII Section A. Officers, Directors, Trustees, Key Employees, and Highest Compensated Employees *(continued)*

(A) Name and title	(B) Average hours per week (list any hours for related organizations below dotted line)	(C) Position (do not check more than one box, unless person is both an officer and a director/trustee)						(D) Reportable compensation from the organization (W-2/1099-MISC)	(E) Reportable compensation from related organizations (W-2/1099-MISC)	(F) Estimated amount of other compensation from the organization and related organizations
		Individual trustee or director	Institutional trustee	Officer	Key employee	Highest compensated employee	Former			
(15)										
(16)										
(17)										
(18)										
(19)										
(20)										
(21)										
(22)										
(23)										
(24)										
(25)										

1b Sub-total . . . . ▶

c Total from continuation sheets to Part VII, Section A . . . . . ▶

d Total (add lines 1b and 1c) . . . . ▶

2 Total number of individuals (including but not limited to those listed above) who received more than $100,000 of reportable compensation from the organization ▶

		Yes	No
3	Did the organization list any **former** officer, director, or trustee, key employee, or highest compensated employee on line 1a? *If "Yes," complete Schedule J for such individual* **3**		
4	For any individual listed on line 1a, is the sum of reportable compensation and other compensation from the organization and related organizations greater than $150,000? *If "Yes," complete Schedule J for such individual* **4**		
5	Did any person listed on line 1a receive or accrue compensation from any unrelated organization or individual for services rendered to the organization? *If "Yes," complete Schedule J for such person* **5**		

Section B. Independent Contractors

1 Complete this table for your five highest compensated independent contractors that received more than $100,000 of compensation from the organization. Report compensation for the calendar year ending with or within the organization's tax year.

(A) Name and business address	(B) Description of services	(C) Compensation

2 Total number of independent contractors (including but not limited to those listed above) who received more than $100,000 of compensation from the organization ▶

Form **990** (2014)

Form 990 (2014)   Page **9**

| Part VIII | Statement of Revenue |

Check if Schedule O contains a response or note to any line in this Part VIII . . . . ☐

			(A) Total revenue	(B) Related or exempt function revenue	(C) Unrelated business revenue	(D) Revenue excluded from tax under sections 512-514
Contributions, Gifts, Grants and Other Similar Amounts	**1a**	Federated campaigns . . .	**1a**			
	b	Membership dues	1b			
	c	Fundraising events	1c			
	d	Related organizations . . .	1d			
	e	Government grants (contributions)	1e			
	f	All other contributions, gifts, grants, and similar amounts not included above	1f			
	g	Noncash contributions included in lines 1a-1f: $				
	h	**Total.** Add lines 1a-1f . . . . ▶				
Program Service Revenue	**2a**	_____	Business Code			
	b	_____				
	c	_____				
	d	_____				
	e	_____				
	f	All other program service revenue .				
	g	**Total.** Add lines 2a-2f . . . . ▶				
Other Revenue	**3**	Investment income (including dividends, interest, and other similar amounts) . . . . . . ▶				
	4	Income from investment of tax-exempt bond proceeds ▶				
	5	Royalties . . . . ▶				
			(i) Real	(ii) Personal		
	6a	Gross rents . .				
	b	Less: rental expenses				
	c	Rental income or (loss)				
	d	Net rental income or (loss) . . . . . . ▶				
	7a	Gross amount from sales of assets other than inventory	(i) Securities	(ii) Other		
	b	Less: cost or other basis and sales expenses .				
	c	Gain or (loss) . . .				
	d	Net gain or (loss) . . . . ▶				
	8a	Gross income from fundraising events (not including $ _____ of contributions reported on line 1c). See Part IV, line 18 . . . . . a				
	b	Less: direct expenses . . . . b				
	c	Net income or (loss) from fundraising events . ▶				
	9a	Gross income from gaming activities. See Part IV, line 19 . . . . . a				
	b	Less: direct expenses . . . . b				
	c	Net income or (loss) from gaming activities . . ▶				
	10a	Gross sales of inventory, less returns and allowances . . . a				
	b	Less: cost of goods sold . . . b				
	c	Net income or (loss) from sales of inventory . . ▶				
		Miscellaneous Revenue	Business Code			
	11a	_____				
	b	_____				
	c	_____				
	d	All other revenue				
	e	**Total.** Add lines 11a-11d . . . . ▶				
	12	**Total revenue.** See instructions. . . . . . ▶				

Form **990** (2014)

Part IX **Statement of Functional Expenses**

Section 501(c)(3) and 501(c)(4) organizations must complete all columns. All other organizations must complete column (A).

Check if Schedule O contains a response or note to any line in this Part IX . . . . ☐

Do not include amounts reported on lines 6b, 7b, 8b, 9b, and 10b of Part VIII.	(A) Total expenses	(B) Program service expenses	(C) Management and general expenses	(D) Fundraising expenses
1 Grants and other assistance to domestic organizations and domestic governments. See Part IV, line 21 . .				
2 Grants and other assistance to domestic individuals. See Part IV, line 22				
3 Grants and other assistance to foreign organizations, foreign governments, and foreign individuals. See Part IV, lines 15 and 16 . . .				
4 Benefits paid to or for members				
5 Compensation of current officers, directors, trustees, and key employees				
6 Compensation not included above, to disqualified persons (as defined under section 4958(f)(1)) and persons described in section 4958(c)(3)(B) . .				
7 Other salaries and wages				
8 Pension plan accruals and contributions (include section 401(k) and 403(b) employer contributions)				
9 Other employee benefits				
10 Payroll taxes				
11 Fees for services (non-employees):				
a Management				
b Legal				
c Accounting				
d Lobbying				
e Professional fundraising services. See Part IV, line 17				
f Investment management fees				
g Other. (If line 11g amount exceeds 10% of line 25, column (A) amount, list line 11g expenses on Schedule O.) . .				
12 Advertising and promotion				
13 Office expenses				
14 Information technology				
15 Royalties				
16 Occupancy				
17 Travel				
18 Payments of travel or entertainment expenses for any federal, state, or local public officials				
19 Conferences, conventions, and meetings .				
20 Interest				
21 Payments to affiliates				
22 Depreciation, depletion, and amortization .				
23 Insurance				
24 Other expenses. Itemize expenses not covered above (List miscellaneous expenses in line 24e. If line 24e amount exceeds 10% of line 25, column (A) amount, list line 24e expenses on Schedule O.)				
a _____				
b _____				
c _____				
d _____				
e All other expenses				
25 Total functional expenses. Add lines 1 through 24e				
26 Joint costs. Complete this line only if the organization reported in column (B) joint costs from a combined educational campaign and fundraising solicitation. Check here ▶ ☐ if following SOP 98-2 (ASC 958-720)				

Form 990 (2014)   Page **11**

Part X   Balance Sheet

Check if Schedule O contains a response or note to any line in this Part X . . . . ☐

			(A) Beginning of year		**(B)** End of year
Assets	1	Cash—non-interest-bearing		1	
	2	Savings and temporary cash investments		2	
	3	Pledges and grants receivable, net		3	
	4	Accounts receivable, net		4	
	5	Loans and other receivables from current and former officers, directors, trustees, key employees, and highest compensated employees. Complete Part II of Schedule L		5	
	6	Loans and other receivables from other disqualified persons (as defined under section 4958(f)(1)), persons described in section 4958(c)(3)(B), and contributing employers and sponsoring organizations of section 501(c)(9) voluntary employees' beneficiary organizations (see instructions). Complete Part II of Schedule L		6	
	7	Notes and loans receivable, net		7	
	8	Inventories for sale or use		8	
	9	Prepaid expenses and deferred charges		9	
	10a	Land, buildings, and equipment: cost or other basis. Complete Part VI of Schedule D 10a			
	b	Less: accumulated depreciation 10b		10c	
	11	Investments—publicly traded securities		11	
	12	Investments—other securities. See Part IV, line 11		12	
	13	Investments—program-related. See Part IV, line 11		13	
	14	Intangible assets		14	
	15	Other assets. See Part IV, line 11		15	
	16	**Total assets.** Add lines 1 through 15 (must equal line 34)		16	
Liabilities	17	Accounts payable and accrued expenses		17	
	18	Grants payable		18	
	19	Deferred revenue		19	
	20	Tax-exempt bond liabilities		20	
	21	Escrow or custodial account liability. Complete Part IV of Schedule D .		21	
	22	Loans and other payables to current and former officers, directors, trustees, key employees, highest compensated employees, and disqualified persons. Complete Part II of Schedule L		22	
	23	Secured mortgages and notes payable to unrelated third parties . .		23	
	24	Unsecured notes and loans payable to unrelated third parties . . .		24	
	25	Other liabilities (including federal income tax, payables to related third parties, and other liabilities not included on lines 17-24). Complete Part X of Schedule D		25	
	26	**Total liabilities.** Add lines 17 through 25		26	
Net Assets or Fund Balances		**Organizations that follow SFAS 117 (ASC 958), check here ▶ ☐ and complete lines 27 through 29, and lines 33 and 34.**			
	27	Unrestricted net assets		27	
	28	Temporarily restricted net assets		28	
	29	Permanently restricted net assets		29	
		Organizations that do not follow SFAS 117 (ASC 958), check here ▶ ☐ and complete lines 30 through 34.			
	30	Capital stock or trust principal, or current funds		30	
	31	Paid-in or capital surplus, or land, building, or equipment fund . . .		31	
	32	Retained earnings, endowment, accumulated income, or other funds .		32	
	33	Total net assets or fund balances		33	
	34	Total liabilities and net assets/fund balances		34	

Form **990** (2014)

Part XI **Reconciliation of Net Assets**

Check if Schedule O contains a response or note to any line in this Part XI . . . . ☐

1	Total revenue (must equal Part VIII, column (A), line 12)	**1**	
2	Total expenses (must equal Part IX, column (A), line 25)	**2**	
3	Revenue less expenses. Subtract line 2 from line 1	**3**	
4	Net assets or fund balances at beginning of year (must equal Part X, line 33, column (A)) . . .	**4**	
5	Net unrealized gains (losses) on investments	**5**	
6	Donated services and use of facilities	**6**	
7	Investment expenses	**7**	
8	Prior period adjustments	**8**	
9	Other changes in net assets or fund balances (explain in Schedule O)	**9**	
10	Net assets or fund balances at end of year. Combine lines 3 through 9 (must equal Part X, line 33, column (B))	**10**	

Part XII **Financial Statements and Reporting**

Check if Schedule O contains a response or note to any line in this Part XII . . . . ☐

		Yes	No
1	Accounting method used to prepare the Form 990: ☐ Cash ☐ Accrual ☐ Other _____ If the organization changed its method of accounting from a prior year or checked "Other," explain in Schedule O.		
2a	Were the organization's financial statements compiled or reviewed by an independent accountant? . . .	**2a**	
	If "Yes," check a box below to indicate whether the financial statements for the year were compiled or reviewed on a separate basis, consolidated basis, or both:		
	☐ Separate basis ☐ Consolidated basis ☐ Both consolidated and separate basis		
b	Were the organization's financial statements audited by an independent accountant?	**2b**	
	If "Yes," check a box below to indicate whether the financial statements for the year were audited on a separate basis, consolidated basis, or both:		
	☐ Separate basis ☐ Consolidated basis ☐ Both consolidated and separate basis		
c	If "Yes" to line 2a or 2b, does the organization have a committee that assumes responsibility for oversight of the audit, review, or compilation of its financial statements and selection of an independent accountant?	**2c**	
	If the organization changed either its oversight process or selection process during the tax year, explain in Schedule O.		
3a	As a result of a federal award, was the organization required to undergo an audit or audits as set forth in the Single Audit Act and OMB Circular A-133?	**3a**	
b	If "Yes," did the organization undergo the required audit or audits? If the organization did not undergo the required audit or audits, explain why in Schedule O and describe any steps taken to undergo such audits.	**3b**	

Form **990** (2014)

153

The 990 core is divided into the following parts:

Part I- Summary Includes mission statement and number of employees and volunteers. Additionally, it presents totals of revenues and expenses by certain types, such as program services and professional fundraising expenses. Totals of assets, liabilities, and net assets or "fund balances" are also required.

Part II- Signature Block This is the regular signature box.

Part III- Statement of Program Service Accomplishments Programs must be presented here with sufficient detail to link them to the mission statement, and to show the IRS and prospective donors that the programs are at the heart of the organization.

Part IV- Checklist of Required Schedules Questionnaire must be answered to determine schedules to be completed. The schedules are detailed, enabling the IRS to evaluate any possible violation of the rules. Additionally, many nonprofits base their own policies and procedures on this schedule.

Part V- Statements Regarding Other IRS Filings and Tax Compliance Checklist shown with potential other compliance requirements not necessarily related to Form 990 itself, such as the number of W-2G filed.

Part VI- Governance, Management, and Disclosure Questions government and management policies, while promoting transparency and accountability. Nonprofits want to respond "yes" to some questions, such as the one asking if the nonprofit has written policies and procedures for chapters to follow, ensuring consistency throughout the organization. Many nonprofits base their policies and procedures on the requirements of this part.

Part VII- Compensation of Officers, Directors, Trustees, Key Employees, Highest Compensated Employees, and Independent Contractors This part reflects the IRS's concern with excessive compensation and benefits. Part VI, lines 15 a and b directly relate to this area. If the organization answered "No" to either question and then shows salaries that are much higher than expected, the nonprofit may receive more scrutiny.

Part VIII- Statement of Revenue Sources of support are presented, including potentially taxable unrelated business income. This statement can be analyzed carefully in case there is too much reliance on a sole source that is easily threatened in a weak economy. The expectation is for unrelated business revenue to be insignificant as compared with other revenues. Excess unrelated business revenue puts the organization at risk of losing its tax exemption. (Donations of services are excluded from this statement.)

Part IX- Statement of Functional Expenses Part IX shows allocation of expenses among program, management, and fundraising expenses. The purpose is to show that the nonprofit has been using revenues properly, i.e., mostly in programs. Sometimes, fundraising or administrative expenses may seem excessive and need to be decreased or justified, such as in a new organization conducting fundraising to pay for programs not yet fully available. (Donations of services are excluded from this statement.)

Part X- Balance Sheet Presents the Statement of Position data with more details, such as loans to officers, directors, and key employees. This part focuses on the liquidity and fiscal stability of a nonprofit.

Part XI- Reconciliation of Net Assets Shows a compilation of revenues, expenses, and other items, such as donated services, to prove that the total net assets number in Part X- Balance Sheet is correct according to the nonprofit's own financial reports.

Part XII- Financial Statements and Reporting This part requires details on the financial statements preparation, such as accounting methods and the work of an independent accountant. Moreover, this part covers audits and Single Audits, making nonprofits aware of those.

The 990 also includes salary information for highly paid executives and consultants. This is not confidential information. Additionally, disclosures related to contractors and consultants are not kept confidential. Because of this lack of privacy, some businesses decide not to apply for tax exemption.

Although 990 or 990-EZ Schedule B requests information about donors, Section 501(c)(3) organizations do not need to make public the names and addresses of contributors included in this schedule.

Note that some organizations use 990s as marketing tools to display their programs and accomplishments. It is common for the 990 to include extensive attachments, showing details of programs and the good they do in the community.

Unrelated Business Income Tax

As mentioned before, nonprofits can have income that is taxed, which is known as Unrelated Business Taxable Income (UBTI). Organizations may owe taxes even if they only file the 990-N form.

If an organization has UBTI of $1,000, it must file 990-T Unrelated Business. The government defines taxable income as income not substantially related to the organization's tax-exempt purposes or activities. The idea is to prevent nonprofit organizations from competing with for-profit entities unfairly. The tax due is known as Unrelated Business Income Tax (UBIT). Often, an activity generates unrelated business income if it meets three requirements:

1. It is a trade or business
2. It is regularly carried on, and
3. It is not substantially related to furthering the exempt purpose of the organization.

For example, a nonprofit organization runs a pizza parlor selling pizza to the public. The nonprofit's mission and programs do not relate to the parlor's business. The nonprofit pays employees to run the pizza place. All this information points to the pizza parlor generating unrelated business income that is taxable.

On the other hand, a humanitarian-service nonprofit holds a bake sale. While the sale is unrelated to the mission, it is likely to be tax-exempt if not "regularly carried on." Nonprofit's activities are considered regularly carried on if they show a frequency, continuity, similarity to comparable commercial activities of for-profit businesses.

Some unrelated business activities may not be taxed. For instance, if an organization sells donated items or if all of the labor involved in the business is performed by volunteers, proceeds are exempt from taxes.

Other Tax Situations

Nonprofit organizations face various tax situations, besides income taxes. Some of these issues are:

Pension Plans

Nonprofits have the choice of offering two types of pension plans: the 403(b), the traditional nonprofit annuity plan, and the 401(k), similar to the for-profit retirement plan. Under both plans, the employee contribution is not taxed; but limits, laws, and regulations are different between these two plans.

Contractors

All nonprofits are required to comply with federal, state, and local laws and regulations. For instance, nonprofits are required to file 1099s related to vendors, just like any other business. Actually, 990-Part V, question 1a reads, "Enter the number reported in Box (3) of Form 1096, Annual Summary and Transmittal of U.S. Information Returns. Enter-0- if not applicable." (The 1096 is the transmittal form for 1099s.)

The IRS has become aware that many organizations do not follow the rules as they should and wants more nonprofits to consider and comply with the 1099/1096 filing requirement.

Sales Tax

Nonprofits could owe sales, excise, or use taxes on fundraising and other revenue-generating events, depending on the state. Each state is different and nonprofits must review the laws before any fundraising activity. Certain exemptions may need to be filed and approved before fundraising events; otherwise, the organization will owe sales tax as per state's laws.

Payroll

Payroll processes for most nonprofits are just like those of for-profits. The Treasury Inspector General for Tax Administration released a report in 2014 called, "Some Tax-Exempt Organizations Have Substantial Delinquent Payroll Taxes." In this report, twenty-five organizations received government payments over a three-year period of $148 million, including Medicare and Medicaid. The nonprofits owned assets of more than $97 million, but did not remit payroll and other taxes, including penalties. You can read this report at the government website: http://www.treasury.gov.

Nonprofits should make sure that all deductions are taken and all taxes are paid. Many times payroll-processing firms are misinformed about payroll responsibilities and process payroll with mistakes. Check with your state about specific state payroll considerations, including unemployment and disability insurance. Double check reports from payroll-processing companies to be sure all tax liabilities are covered.

An interesting topic for nonprofits is the issue of employees required to work as volunteers. This can be sticky. If anybody is required to volunteer, then it is not really volunteering, and employees could be eligible for overtime pay. If the organization does not pay up, it may be in trouble legally. I suggest not requiring employees to volunteer, and to pay them if they do; in the case of exempt employees, give them paid time-off credits for the volunteering time.

The IRS and state governments do not allow nonprofits or for-profits to treat employees as independent contractors. Some of the rules to determine if someone is an employee or contractor are:

1. Behavioral: Does the company control or have the right to control what the worker does and how the worker does his or her job?
2. Financial: Are the business aspects of the worker's job

controlled by the payer? (These include things like how the worker is paid, whether expenses are reimbursed, who provides tools/supplies, etc.).

3. Type of Relationship: Are there written contracts or employee-type benefits (i.e., pension plan, insurance, vacation pay, etc.)? Will the relationship continue and is the work performed a key aspect of the business?

The more positive responses, the more it is likely that the person is an employee of the nonprofit, not a contractor. In case of an audit, the organization will be liable for taxes, interest, and penalties on employees classified incorrectly as contractors. This can be expensive.

Excise Tax

The IRS has established "intermediate sanctions" to handle situations where private inurement is present, but it does not warrant the loss of the tax exemption. The sanction, known as the excise tax, starts at 25 percent of the excess benefit and is imposed on the person who received the benefit. There is also a fine to the organization manager involved in the transaction.

An example of private inurement is if someone from a board of directors, or his/her relative, buys a house for $10 from the organization. The person was in a position of power and used it for his/her own benefit. The excise tax would be 25 percent of the value of the home, less the $10. The board member could also be liable for the fine as an organization manager.

<u>Summary</u>

Most tax-exempt organizations need to file 990 tax returns at the federal level, including the 990-N, the e-card filed online by small nonprofits. Forms 990 and 990-EZ request detailed information about the nonprofit, such as mission statement, revenues and expenses, and program descriptions.

Organizations liable for income taxes on unrelated business income should file 990-T to report and pay taxes related to these transactions. The idea is to avoid giving nonprofits an unfair business advantage.

Other tax compliance issues concerning nonprofits are payroll, sales tax, and contractor identification and reporting. In some cases, excise taxes are also applied to certain individuals within the nonprofit organization.

9

Internal Controls

"Quality is not an act. It is a habit."

Aristotle

Concepts of internal controls are not new; they have existed for many years. Internal controls focus on checks and balances, ethics, proper governance, responsibility, and accountability for financial information. The goals here are to prevent losses and improve the reliability and quality of fiscal reporting.

Since every nonprofit is different, the internal control practices are likely to vary. However, there is guidance to internal control issues and processes, such as the Sarbanes and Oxley Act at the federal level, and state law requirements similar to the "Nonprofit Integrity Act of 2004" of California.

In addition, the Committee of Sponsoring Organizations (COSO) of the Treadway Commission has promulgated a well-known integrated framework for firms to follow when considering internal controls in general.

The IRS is also interested in having nonprofits implement procedures to decrease fraud and losses, while improving efficiencies. To this end, certain questions on the 990 tax return give clues about some governance controls expected, such as:

- o Does the organization have a written conflict of interest policy?

- o Are officers, directors, or trustees and key employees required to disclose interests that could give rise to conflicts?

- o Does the organization regularly and consistently monitor and enforce compliance with policy? If "Yes," describe in Schedule O how this is done.

- o Does the organization have a written whistleblower policy?

- o Does the organization have a written document-retention and destruction policy?

These questions are supposed to be answered in the affirmative by nonprofits, confirming these controls. At the very least, the nonprofits become aware of expected internal controls practices that should be seriously considered.

While many organizations base their checks and balances on tax returns, these are not the only procedures available to help nonprofits monitor their daily operations. The idea is to examine a task, identify risks, and create preventive control procedures to eliminate or at least minimize such risks.

Internal controls do not need to be complicated or expensive. Small organizations can utilize common processes, such as conducting monthly bank reconciliations to identify problem areas. Having someone from the board or the executive director take a look at bank transactions online can also be an effective procedure to identify many fiscal issues.

Unfortunately, some nonprofits consider controls only after serious problems happen, such as large losses due to errors or fraud. This type of attitude must change; nonprofits need to be proactive about implementing proper procedures to avoid problems and not just react to issues as they happen.

Common Internal Control Practices

Some internal control practices are very popular within the nonprofit sector, helping in management and grant compliance. These are usually incorporated in the policies and procedures documentation, including specific practices to minimize errors and losses.

Not only is it important for nonprofits to implement these practices, but they must also maintain them to obtain full benefits. If procedures are followed only occasionally, the nonprofit will still be at risk for fraud and errors. Therefore, as part of any internal control practice, there must be a mechanism to be sure they are indeed followed, such as using checklists and management supervision.

Segregation of Duties

Segregation of duties involves the separation of certain activities to decrease errors and theft. The idea is to have more than one person involved in certain tasks, so if errors or fraud occurs on one step, the problem may be picked up on in another. In general, segregation of duties involves the separation of three functions:

- Custody of assets
- Authorization or approval of related transactions affecting those assets
- Recording or reporting of related transactions.

For example, the person who sends out invoices should not be involved in the receipt of money. If the same person were to handle these activities, he/she is in the position to potentially pocket the money and delete/credit the invoice from the system without anybody noticing the theft. Errors may also not be caught and fixed if one person does all the processes, putting at risk the integrity of the information.

Following the same concept, only certain non-accounting people should initiate and approve discounts. Otherwise, anybody, including accounting personnel, may give big discounts to friends and family and would be capable of receiving kickbacks from customers in exchange for hefty discounts with nobody else noticing the problem.

✓ **A traditional feature of segregation of duties is for the person who pays the bills not to sign the payment checks.**

Managers not involved with accounting typically sign the checks. This may be a CFO, if the nonprofit is large and this person is not involved in the daily accounting activities. The payments are presented for signature along with backup documentation, so that the signor can review it before signing the checks.

If segregation of duties is not possible, which is often the case in smaller organizations, other controls can be in place to minimize the risks. For example, the treasurer or someone from the board could login the bank website online and take a look at bank transactions once a week. Someone from the board may also review bank reconciliations and lists of new vendors generated by the accounting system. Any odd vendor or amount can be identified, minimizing the risk of payments to fake vendors.

Computerized Systems

As software and computer costs have decreased, many nonprofits use computerized systems that are quite sophisticated. Such systems not only help in calculations and reporting, but also in the safekeeping of fiscal data. Usually, the information is backed up daily and can be retrieved without much effort. This is a major advantage over paper-and-pencil systems, where pages can be lost and damaged easily. Unless copies were made of the paper ledgers, all information may be lost, causing delays and extra costs to replace the missing data manually. With a computerized system, some data may be lost, but it is usually a much more contained situation.

Computerized systems also help with security and internal controls because they require IDs and passwords. Rights are given to users, who access certain sections of the programs and not others. For instance, the accounts payable clerk should enter only that area and not others, reducing the risk of errors and leaks of confidential information

Advanced fiscal systems may allow for approvals on invoices online, saving time and streamlining the process. Sometimes such programs interface with a time sheet and/or customer service software, making it very efficient in capturing data without human errors.

Written documentation from temporarily and permanently restricted donations must be kept separate in a safe location. Some nonprofits scan these documents, so that if papers are lost, they retain records of the gifts on the long-term basis.

Policies and Procedures (P&Ps)

Nonprofits create policies and procedures to influence and control major decisions and behavior, so they take place within acceptable boundaries. P&Ps are usually based on internal control principles, mission statement, laws, and regulations. Many organizations use the tax returns questions to identity areas where P&Ps will be beneficial in improving internal controls.

Policies are general in nature, presenting guidelines based on the organization's mission and values. For example, a policy could be implemented to discontinue fundraising contact with any person who requested it orally or in writing. Based on this policy nonprofits may create various procedures to achieve this goal.

Procedures are specific, including steps, methods, and actions designed to implement a policy. It is common for a policy to include many procedures. Sometimes the procedures are so detailed they can be employed as a manual, while at other times, manuals are created from procedures, but contain more detailed information, such as print screens of some programs.

Together, the P&Ps unify the culture of an organization, simplifying decision making and setting the tone at the top. To this end, nonprofit organizations often implement a number classification to structure the documentation. For example, P&Ps for the accounting department could be identified by the Section 300. If someone looks for a procedure related to assets, he/she would go to the Section 300, limiting confusion. Many nonprofits also include a table of contents to facilitate research and consulting of P&Ps.

Code of Conduct

A code of conduct encompasses rules outlining proper practices and responsibilities of the nonprofit, including the board of directors and management. Such code often includes ethical and moral behavior to be followed by everyone, not just clerical or low level employees. It is based on the mission statement of the organization and all employees and directors are often required to sign confirming having read it.

The values of honesty and integrity are often mentioned in codes of conduct along with unacceptable behaviors, such as sexual harassment. This document may mention inappropriate language in business communications and conduct, along with unsuitable pictures displays. It may comment on confidentiality, conflicts of interest, outside activities, and relationships with vendors and suppliers. Often it also contains prohibitions against kickbacks and secret commissions. Many nonprofit organizations post their codes of conduct on their websites, such as the Independent Sector at www.independentsector.org/code_of_ethics

Many important guidelines mention a code of conduct for a business, including the Sarbanes and Oxley Act, the Super Circular, and even the tax Form 990. The idea is for nonprofits to implement such code and not treat it as "lip service."

Specific Control Features

Traditionally, many nonprofits use certain controls to protect risky functions, such as cash transactions. However, there are some controls used in all sections of an organization, such as the requirement for all employees to take vacations (fraud and other problems are usually found when the employee is away). Next are some common nonprofit risks and controls in various areas.

Cash- Receivables- Revenue

Cash is not simply money, but also checks and credit card payments required to maintain programs and pay its bills. Some key risks and controls with cash, receivables/revenue are discussed next.

Risk: Cash/checks can be lost or stolen.

This is a major risk for any nonprofit. As a control mechanism, two people should count cash before it is deposited to be sure the total is correct. In addition, nonprofits should acquire a safe preferably bolted into the wall or floor with the code known to limited personnel to safeguard cash, checks not yet deposited, and other valuables. Another control is to limit physical access to the area where money is received to just a few people.

Do not keep cash, checks, or credit card slips in a desk or in another unsafe place that is easily accessible. Thieves typically look for petty cash in drawers under desks.

As a control mechanism, nonprofits should use their websites to collect money as much as possible. Additionally, they could implement a policy indicating that no cash over a certain amount would be accepted to minimize the risk for losses. If money is received, it must be deposited promptly in the bank after being counted by two separate individuals to confirm the amount of cash. A nonprofit I know lost over $12,000 in cash brought to the premises. Somehow the money never made it to the bank, and it was unclear what happened or who was responsible for the loss. Soon after that, the nonprofit decided not to accept any hard cash over $100 from anybody.

A traditional cash control is for nonprofits to perform bank reconciliations, also known as cash reconciliations, every month to be sure all cash transactions have been accounted for properly. Reconciliations can be deterrents to cash theft. If people are aware of cash being monitored and reconciled, they might think twice before trying to "borrow" money. Errors can be found as well by using reconciliations; for example, if the accounting records include a check for $30, but the bank shows that same check as $300, then there is an error to be fixed at the nonprofit's ledger or at the bank's side, depending on the situation.

Moreover, phone calls or emails with complaints about payments not showing up on statements or invoices are good controls for cash. It's best for these calls to be forwarded to someone not involved with accounts receivable for follow up. The problem could be just an erro,r or an unfortunate situation where money was stolen.

Risk: Unauthorized credits/bad debt write-offs can be applied to receivables.

This risk often goes together with loss of cash. Someone might receive payment in full, but instead of showing the payment, the person steals part or the full amount, giving a credit, or a write-off to the account in the accounting system.

Controls to avoid this problem include segregation of duties, where the person who is in charge of accounts receivable does not handle money received by the nonprofit, as mentioned earlier. Another control would be for all write-offs and credits to be initiated and approved by individuals outside the accounts receivable section, such as the executive director or a development manager.

Risk: Numbers for cash, accounts receivable, and revenues could be wrong.

Managers can identify this problem by reviewing an "accounts receivable aging report," a summary of the receivable details, also known as a "subsidiary ledger." Total in this report should agree with the number shown in the financial statements. Many nonprofits' accountants run and print aging reports as part of their "closing" each accounting period.

Errors may happen for various reasons. Sometimes mistakes occur when entries bypass the individual donor/member individual account. Instead of applying a payment to each individual subsidiary account, the accountant may apply the amount directly to the general ledger, used to compile financial reports. Other times, the individual donor record is correct, but because of a glitch, the system does not transfer to the general ledger. Controls for these problems involve, again, monthly bank reconciliations along with comparisons between the numbers in the aging reports and the ones in the general ledger.

Sometimes errors happen because of duplicate invoices sent out. A control for this risk is to centralize the invoicing function in one place, so that one report can be reviewed with an eye toward identification and correction of possible duplicate invoices. Fundraising departments may send out invoices outside the accounting system, while the accounting department also sends out its own bills, creating duplication and confusion. Better to let only the accounting department do the invoicing process, since it is the area best equipped to deal with this issue.

Accounts Payable- Expenses

Accounts payable is part of any business, including nonprofits. Not only do bills need to be approved and paid, but in the nonprofit world, they also need to be coded by area, program, and grant, making the recognition of each expense quite complex. Some key risks and controls with accounts payable-expenses are the following:

Risk: Unauthorized payments occur.

To avoid the risk of unauthorized payments, managers should approve all invoices, even if the costs are budgeted. Accounting department staff must be skeptical of all bills received and pay them only when they are approved. To speed up this process, management could approve a "hot list" for utilities and other regular bills that may be paid without authorization, provided they are reasonable when compared with past expenses.

Payments to fake vendors can be minimized by a supervisor review of "change/add vendor" reports regularly, as these reports are available in many computer systems. The person signing the checks can also identify unauthorized payments if he/she takes a close look at the backup documentation.

Since banking is often done on the Internet these days, if payments are made online using the bank website, a control may be for the bank to send an email to the executive director immediately after each online payment transaction. Another control involving the bank is to require two authorizations on any wire transfers.

To detect unauthorized problems, someone separate from the accounting tasks could log in the bank website and review payments online regularly. Just knowing that someone will review online transactions at least once a week can be a deterrent to fraud.

Risk: Checks are changed after signed.

To avoid this risk, banks offer pre-approved list services, where checks are paid only if the payee and the amount on the checks agree with the ones on the listing. This service prevents checks that may have been stolen or modified from being paid. For example, if a check is presented for payment for $1,000, but is listed as $100, the bank will not honor it and will call the nonprofit regarding the payment. Sometimes accounting makes mistakes and checks are changed. In this case, the staff needs to notify the bank about the error. This service can be expensive but may be worthwhile.

Nonprofits must keep its check stock safe in a locked place. They should also protect voided checks by keeping them in a safe place along with backup documentation. Only a few accounting employees would have access to these items.

Bank reconciliations could pick up this issue, since the number on the accounting system may be different from the number on bank statements. However, this control may not be that effective because by the time reconciliations are done, the person may have deposited or cashed the check and be gone with the money.

Moreover, someone separate from the accounting department logging in and reviewing payments online in the bank website regularly can detect the problem. This person is likely to identify odd vendors and amounts and provides an extra layer of control.

Risk: Double-paying vendors.

Nonprofits can minimize this common problem by using a computerized system that does not allow for duplicate invoice numbers. In addition, nonprofits should implement a policy of paying invoices only and not statements, which may be filed for information only.

A traditional control is for accounting staff to stamp the invoices "Paid" so they do not pay the expense again. Paid invoices can be marked as such in the computerized accounting system, in case the invoices are scanned and kept in a virtual environment.

Another control mechanism is for the controller or accounting manager to review the accounts payable master list of vendors monthly to identify double entries of vendors. For example, a company may be listed as Ammy's Plumbing and as Amy's Plumbing in the accounting system. A payment went out under Ammy's name. Now suppose the vendor calls and the person looks up Amy's Plumbing, sees no payments, and generates another payment under that name, creating a duplicate check for the same vendor. This is easy to do when a master list has duplicate vendors.

Risk: Losing bills and paying late fees.

To prevent this problem, all bills should be forwarded to the accounting department, whose staff stamp them with date received. It is common for vendors to send bills to specific people before going to the finance department. These bills cannot be put inside a drawer and forgotten until weeks later. They must be forwarded to accounting right away.

In addition, some bills may be paid late because they were emailed to certain people, and they may be away or no longer working for the organization. These vendors must be identified and contacted with an updated contact email address.

Risk: Being a victim of scams.

Be aware of scam artists focusing on nonprofits. I witnessed a fraud in a nonprofit organization involving printer cartridges. The deal was to mail out bad cartridges and then send a bill for payment. Nobody really ordered the cartridges, but the scammer had a name of someone in administration who supposedly ordered the items. In this case, the person had left the nonprofit many months before and could not have ordered anything. The sale was also not authorized by any managers, who knew nothing about the deal. Nonprofits must have a strong authorization control system to be able to avoid scams like this.

✓ Visit http://www.FTC.gov frequently, looking out for scams.

Another known fraud is someone stealing a credit card, making a large donation online, and then requesting a refund on another card or a check for the money he/she supposedly donated. By the time the organization notices the problem, it may be too late and the money is gone.

A control for scams is for the accounting department staff and others to be on alert when they receive a bill, a mysterious delivery, or an odd request for reimbursement. I witnessed an accounts payable accountant pay all bills received regardless of approvals because she was concerned about late payments. This is not a good strategy.

Risk: Numbers for accounts payable and expenses could be wrong.

An issue with computerized systems is that the number showing up on financial reports may not be right. A manager can identify this problem by running an "accounts payable aging report" and comparing the total number on this report with the one on financial statements. They should agree. It does not make sense for a Statement of Position to show $300 in liabilities, while the payable aging report shows only $100; but it happens.

Sometimes errors occur when entries bypass the individual vendor account. Other times, the individual vendor ledger is correct, but a glitch prevents all information from being transferred to the general ledger, the basis for the financial statements.

Another type of error is input mistake when entering bills in the system. A good way to avoid this problem is to add up all the bills to be entered first, and then compare the number with a report of all invoices entered from the system. The numbers should agree, and if not, accounting personnel must find and correct any errors.

Controls for accuracy problems also include bank reconciliations, where numbers on bank statements are compared with the ones on the accounting system. If they are different, it is a sign that something may be wrong with the payables/expenses on the financial reports. Checks listed as outstanding (not yet cashed) should be reviewed with a focus on payments that have not been cashed for a while. These checks may be lost and need to be voided and/or replaced. Many states, such as California, require that "stale"(old) checks be forwarded to them once the check goes uncashed for too long. Nonprofits should contact their states for more information on this topic.

Payroll

Some organizations run on volunteers only, but many need employees to perform certain tasks. Since having employees is costly, it is no surprise that payroll is the biggest expense in the financial statements. Running payroll can be difficult, and while many organizations use outside payroll services, some prefer to process it in-house. Some key risks and controls with payroll are:

Risk: Time sheets could contain wrong information.

In many organizations receiving government funds, everyone files time sheets—even the president—to support charging grants "real" salaries rather than estimated/budgeted ones. Fortunately, many organizations use electronic, computerized timekeeping devices and electronic time sheets that once implemented, reduce errors and confusion significantly.

A traditional internal control is for nonprofits to require supervisory approvals on time sheets (manual or electronic) to make sure hours and overtime are authorized. This feature is typically evaluated by auditors, who verify if the time worked charged to a grant was allocated and authorized properly. If the auditor finds errors or no time sheets, or time sheets with no approvals, the scope of the audit is likely to increase, becoming more expensive.

Risk: Employees may be fictitious.

Each employee should file the proper paperwork with human resources and should visit the HR department personally. I know of a case where a program supervisor "hired" a relative part-time who was a "ghost employee." The nonprofit paid the "employee" for six months, while the supervisor cashed the paychecks. It was only after a problem with the time sheet of this person (all fake) that the human resources manager got involved, and the fraud was discovered. It is crucial for HR to see and meet with all employees, including part-timers to be sure they are real and are actually working for the organization.

Risk: Unauthorized payroll changes or increases happen.

To make sure payroll records are correct, department managers/ directors should review and sign off payroll registers regarding their department at least once a quarter. Many department managers get the dollar amount of their department's payroll expenses through internal regular reporting, but not the details. Therefore, having them verify employees working in each department, sick days, vacations, etc. is very helpful in keeping payroll correct.

Furthermore, controllers should review payroll registers and change reports to make sure the persons running payroll are not paying themselves unauthorized overtime or salary increases—a fraud I witnessed at a nonprofit that could have been prevented had the controller taken a look at payroll reports regularly.

Risk: Paying terminated employees by mistake.

One issue I see often with payroll relates to nonprofits paying terminated employees because payroll did not know about the terminations. It is important for human resources and managers to notify the payroll department when people quit or are let go. Staff may need to process final checks and update the payroll system.

Nonprofits may implement policies and procedures, including a checklist to follow when employees leave or are let go. Many details are involved, such as COBRA requirements that need to be handled properly or the nonprofit could be liable for fines.

Risk: Payroll information may leak.

Confidentiality is important with payroll records. Nonprofits must keep all payroll-related documents, including time sheets, in safe, locked filing cabinets where only a few selected authorized personnel are allowed. Similar security measures should be considered with access to the computerized payroll systems that should be very limited.

In addition, nonprofits should hire people who are discreet and do not discuss confidential matters with others in the organization. They should avoid using email when mentioning any confidential payroll information because the system may not be secure enough.

Information Systems

Many nonprofits keep confidential information in their computers, including sensitive data and items that cannot be lost. Therefore, security and controls involving information systems are necessary concerning the safety of servers, computers, printers, and integrity of data. A typical control of information systems is to have a disaster preparedness plan, which includes a recovery strategy for the nonprofit's functions. However, that is not the only control used in this area. Information system controls can be reviewed as related to software and hardware, including the cloud, as discussed next.

Software

Risks when dealing with software include unauthorized entry, loss of data, and confidentiality issues. Some internal control mechanisms to minimize these risks are:

- Use anti-virus programs to prevent malware from infiltrating the system.
- Do daily backups of all systems and keep the backed up file outside the premises.
- Require IDs and passwords on all systems.
- Acquire programs to identify and stop unauthorized entry using the Internet and other means.
- Require information system's authorization for program purchases to be sure the program is indeed needed and is compatible with existing software.
- Include security to prevent information systems personnel access to password or confidential information.
- Create policies and procedures about computer usage and safety.

Hardware

The risks with hardware involve theft, maintenance, and obsolescence of the machines. Below are some controls to minimize these risks:

- Place all equipment, including servers and printers, in a safe location.
- Label all equipment with numbers and create a list of all equipment using the number and description.
- Maintain this list, doing physical audits to identify equipment disappearances, losses and damages.
- Centralize maintenance services and schedule them regularly.
- Purchases and retirement or sales of old hardware should be approved by information systems management.
- Dispositions of old computers must be done carefully, since they contain confidential information. Files can be recovered

from hard drives, unless the nonprofit takes certain precautions.

Using the Cloud

Many nonprofits have been using accounting and other programs "in the cloud." This means that organizations' management and staff access these computerized programs through the Internet, making the software very convenient since employees can use the system anywhere as long as they have proper online connections, login IDs, and passwords. Organizations using old, unreliable equipment may benefit from the cloud since the data is not saved locally. If the server or individual computers stop working, the information is not lost and is available to the nonprofit.

However, there are risks associated with the cloud system. For example, the program may not be available online for long periods. So, before selecting a cloud system, check its reliability through Internet searches and word-of-mouth.

Once the nonprofit decides to go online, management must trust the Internet provider to provide adequate security for the data, which may include donor information. Not surprisingly, data security of cloud systems is a major concern for both for-profit and nonprofit users.

Another issue with the cloud is the data transfer. If a nonprofit uses the cloud and then moves to another system, the existing data will need to be downloaded and transferred to another program. The cloud provider should allow for such transfers and help the organization in this matter, but some charge fees, so inquiries about this matter are beneficial to avoid surprises later.

<u>**Summary**</u>

Nonprofits employ internal controls to minimize errors and losses in its operations. These procedures, evaluated by auditors, often involve segregation of duties.

Each nonprofit is different, but some common risks identified, such as cash theft, affect many organizations. Once risks are evaluated, controls are set up to minimize them. Monthly reconciliations, written management authorizations, and daily systems' backups are some of the controls employed by nonprofits to manage their risks.

10

Special Considerations

"Helping people doesn't have to be an unsound financial strategy."

Melinda Gates

Nonprofits have many issues that must be considered by managers and boards of directors, such as joint costs, budgeting, and human resources matters. While some of these issues also occur with for-profit businesses, they take on a different aspect when dealing with organizations whose main goal is not to generate profits.

When dealing with special considerations for nonprofits, we must keep in mind that nonprofits focus on programs, the reason for the organizations to be in business. We must also keep in mind that nonprofits rely on public assistance, such as government grants and donations and must use such resources wisely in order to be viable on the long-term basis.

Joint Costs

One of the issues of expense allocation is "joint costs," which relate to the combination of fundraising costs and at least costs in one more area, such as programs or administration. For example, a brochure could include elements of both fundraising and programs. This is an important topic because traditionally nonprofits prefer to allocate the most to programs and the least to fundraising. Why? Because of the expectation that an organization would show less expenses in fundraising than in programs.

Fundraising cost allocation issues were addressed by the AICPA Statement of Position 98-2, "Accounting for Costs of Activities of Not-for-Profit Organizations and State and Local Governmental Entities." The contents of this publication are now part of FASB ASC Subtopic 958-720, Not-for-Profit Entities–Other Expenses. This guideline provides a three-criterion frame of reference and requires that allocations be rational and systematic in its approach to joint costs. The nonprofit must comply with the standards, in this specific order, to qualify for allocation.

1. Purpose of the event
2. Audience
3. Content

The FASB ASC mentions specific requirements within each of this criterion to determine whether costs are all allocated to fundraising or not. This can be tricky. If mailings contain a call for action, such as taking care of a health issue, promoting the nonprofit's mission, then the costs could pass the "purpose" test due to including a programmatic element. If the mailing provides information only, then the costs are fundraising only.

To pass the audience test, nonprofits cannot send mailings to prior donors only or to primarily prior donors. If the organization does that, all the costs are classified as fundraising.

A nonprofit meets the criterion for content if the joint activity supports specific programs or G&A. For example, nonprofits may include financial statements to connect the mailing with G&A and qualify for joint costs.

✓ **Joint costs are mentioned on the 990 tax returns under Part IX- Statement of Functional Expenses**

Interestingly, the standard does not specify the method for allocating costs other than that the method should be rational and systematic. Note that the Statement of Functional Expenses presents joint costs in detail after the allocation.

Budget

It is crucial for a nonprofit to implement an annual budget, an estimate of future revenues and expenses. It is the map to keep the organization in line with its goals and to manage expenses. Without a budget, an organization would be swimming in the dark with nothing to indicate if things are going according to plan or not.

The budget, which must be approved by the board of directors, is also a good internal control tool, helping to identify errors in accounting. For example, if there is a big unexpected variance in a line-item budget, it could be because of an input or reporting mistake that can be corrected.

Nonprofits create budgets based on history and information available at the time. Usually, it does not make sense to create a budget too early. I witnessed organizations creating budgets for board approval six months before the year-end, and that did not work well. Too many things happened in six months, and the budget had to be totally redone a month before the new fiscal year. A budget created within the last two to three months of a prior year is often better and more realistic to be used in the following year.

Many nonprofits have a five-year plan with budget numbers attached to it. This plan is re-visited often to be sure it still make sense and to make adjustments as needed. Besides this long-term document, budgets are usually prepared for one fiscal year and are static throughout the year; however, many times, a "forecasted" amount is used to capture current information.

Once approved by the board, the budget numbers are input into the accounting system for reports showing "actual versus budgeted" numbers throughout the year. Such reports are used by management to make sound decisions.

Some small nonprofits use prior year's revenues and expenses as budgets for the current year. This is better than no budget, but it does not give the nonprofit enough guidance for the future. An organization could start with prior years' revenues and expenses, but should modify them to show a more realistic view of the nonprofit future. For instance, if supplies expense for year was $1,000, and a couple of programs will be cut, then the budget for the future year could show an amount smaller than $1,000.

Often, nonprofits prepare estimated numbers based on accrual or cash bases. Some organizations do both budgets to manage cash during the year. The accrual basis budget recognizes revenues and expenses when they occur, not when they are paid. The cash basis recognizes revenues and expenses when money exchanges hands. Both budget views are valuable.

The issue with budgets is to make sure all expenses are covered by funding sources. When all costs are not covered 100 percent by grants, the nonprofit must seek additional money through fundraising efforts. The best way to do this is to plan and know how much the nonprofit is supposed to raise for the year before it runs out of money.

Another issue with budgets is that no expense can be funded by two or more sources; "double-dipping" is not allowed. For example, a cost for $40 should be reimbursed by one source, not two. If the nonprofit submits the same expense twice, it will be reimbursed twice for one cost, "profiting" from the situation. A well-designed accounting system helps in this situation, where a cost is shown only in accounts or reports for one grant, not multiple ones.

Besides the regular nonprofit budget, many organizations also implement grant budgets that work in parallel with the regular budget. The advantage of this system is that it allows for easy reporting on grant activities, which may run for more than one year, while the regular accounting budget is set up for one year only.

Nonprofit Issues

Nonprofits possess some inherent issues that must be considered by management or donors. These are discussed next.

Tax Exemption

Once an organization receives the 501(c)(3) tax-exempt status, it needs to maintain it. According to the IRS, organizations can risk their tax-exempt status if they engage in certain transactions, such as:

- **Private benefit/inurement:** This issue is about private benefit versus public benefit. The exempt organization should serve the public, not a private individual. Examples are excessive salaries or transfers of property to insiders for less than fair market value.
- **Lobbying:** There are limitations to the amount of lobbying a 501(c)(3) can do. If it affects legislation and is substantial, lobbying can jeopardize the 501(c)(3) status of the organization.
- **Political campaign activity:** Organizations are not to engage in

any political campaign activity; they should not make donations or be involved in it.

- **Activities generating excessive unrelated business income:** Donations and other funds received are exempt from federal taxes, but certain activities not related to the organization's mission are taxed. Examples include sales commissions and membership list sales. When these become excessive, the IRS may question the organization's tax-exempt status.
- **Failure to file appropriate tax returns for 3 years:** Not filing tax returns is grounds for revocation of tax-exempt status.

The IRS can make mistakes, which may cost nonprofits their tax exemption. I know of one nonprofit that lost its tax exemption a few months after getting it. There were no letters about it. The only sign of loss of tax exemption was that the organization was not on the IRS master database and could not file their annual taxes online. Many letters were sent out and a few calls were made to the IRS to correct the situation without success. Finally, the Taxpayer Assistance Program corrected the problem. I highly recommend this program to any nonprofit experiencing unresolved issues with the IRS.

Pledges

Like for-profits, nonprofits utilize accounts receivable; however, unlike for-profits, the receivables are likely to be pledges and grants receivable. Nonprofits often cannot collect on a few pledges, but there is no legal recourse. When there is legal recourse, it is usually not good for the organization's image. Pledges receivable are not as safe and predictable as regular accounts receivable, especially long-term pledges. The risk for default may be high and should be monitored with phone calls and reminders to donors.

If donors pay on pledges using stocks, the risk is that the value of the stock would not be high enough to cover the entire promise. The pledge itself might be decreased, or the donor may need to pay for the difference. This can be tricky.

Human Resources

Hiring and keeping good employees is a challenge faced by most nonprofits. Many cannot compete based on salary amounts. It also may be difficult to hire new employees because the nonprofit sector may not be "sexy" enough.

Another issue is that some jobs may be funded one year and not the following year, creating instability and morale problems within the organization. Additionally, some nonprofits may not be located in a prime neighborhood, nor offer an attractive work environment, making the hiring and retention of employees a bit difficult.

So how can an organization attract and keep good employees?

Some ideas are:

- Generous time-off policy
- Flexible working hours
- Possibility for employees to work from home
- Assistance with transportation
- Opportunities for professional development
- Lots of heartfelt praise
- Possibility of student loan forgiveness when graduates work with certain nonprofits
- Referral program to other nonprofits, if funds are cut and employees are laid off

Nonprofit Resources

Helpful organizations' websites:

Journal of Philanthropy:
http://philanthropy.com/

Idealist:
http://www.idealist.org/

American Society of Association Executives:
http://www.asaecenter.org/

California Association of Nonprofits:
http://calnonprofits.org/

National Council of Non-profit Association:
http://www.councilofnonprofits.org/

AICPA offers conferences, tool kits for boards, etc.:
http://www.aicpa.org

The Nonprofit Resource Center:
http://www.nprcenter.org/

Summary

Nonprofit organizations have their unique situations that should be considered, such as the concept of joint costs, where expenses may be allocated to fundraising & programs, or fundraising & administration. Another issue is the budget preparation and reporting. Without a budget, management is shooting in the dark.

There are a few matters inherent with the nonprofit sector, such as the possibility of losing tax exemption and the instability of pledge collections. Additionally, organizations must be aware of issues in attracting and keeping good employees to take the organization to the next level.

Sheila Shanker

Conclusion

On a final note, dealing with nonprofits can be a challenge, but it can be very rewarding as well. The nonprofit sector badly needs qualified people—those with not only good intentions and hearts, but also with good technical skills, such as educated management, administrative, fundraising, and finance professionals. I hope that this book has inspired these professionals to join the nonprofit sector.

I also hope this book gives you a general roadmap to the nonprofits' issues and peculiarities. The similarities to the for-profit sector are many, but the twists may confuse many professionals, even those with many years of overall experience.

Usually, the confusion starts with the nonprofit's vocabulary. For example, after reading this book and understanding the term "temporarily restricted funds," you will be equipped to have an informed discussion about financial matters.

I trust that this book will help the overwhelmed finance professional or the new member of a board of directors to understand the industry better.

Best wishes in dealing with the nonprofit world!

About the Author

Sheila Shanker is a CPA and MBA based in Culver City, sunny Southern California, where she lives with her husband, a nice old dog and a demanding cat. She has been the Treasurer, Director of Finance and Controller for many organizations.

Sheila's long experience in the nonprofit sector has given her the inside track on what nonprofits are really like, and what the finance professional and board member must know regarding accounting and financial reports. As a consultant, Sheila has helped many organizations in the finance and management areas.

Her first book, "Guide to Nonprofits from the Trenches," published in 2009, was very well received by the nonprofit and accounting communities. A prolific writer, Sheila has over 200 articles published in print and online, including articles at the "Nonprofit Times" and "Journal of Accountancy."

Sheila's background includes teaching online at the MBA program of the University of Liverpool (AACSB accredited). She also enjoys creating online courses, and conducting "live" classes and workshops. You can contact her through her website, www.webshanker.com.

Sheila Shanker

Glossary

Accounting	A systematic way of recording and summarizing financial transactions. It includes reporting and analysis.
Asset	Property owned that can be turned into cash.
Balance Sheet	For-profit financial report that summarizes assets, liabilities, and equity.
Chart of Accounts	A list of all account numbers and descriptions of a business.
Cost Allocation Plan	A fiscal plan presented to a government agency to obtain funding and indirect cost rate for grants.
Determination Letter	A formal IRS letter proving that a nonprofit is indeed tax-exempt.
Direct Costs	Costs relating directly to a program, such as materials spent on an arts program only.
FASB	Financial Accounting Standards Board is a U.S. agency that establishes and communicates accounting principles employed in the U.S.
GAAP	Generally Accepted Accounting Principles is a framework of accounting standards and rules established by the accounting industry in the U.S.
General Ledger	List of all accounts and financial transactions of a business. It is the core of any accounting system.
Income Statement	For-profit financial report summarizing revenues and expenses.
Indirect Costs	Costs relating indirectly to a program, such as insurance of a multipurpose building.
Joint Costs	Costs linked to activities involving fundraising and at least one more area of the organization.
Journal Entries	Mechanism used to log transactions into the accounting books, increasing or decreasing accounts' balances.
Liability	Money or service owed to another party.

Net Asset	Entity that accumulates and classifies transactions, similar to a fund.
Net Assets Released from Restriction	The mechanism employed to transfer revenues from a restricted net asset to an unrestricted one.
Permanently Restricted Net Asset	Net asset that accumulates revenues permanently restricted by donors. Also known as endowment.
Statement of Activities	Nonprofit financial report summarizing revenues and expenses.
Statement of Cash Flows	Financial report of both for-profit and nonprofit organizations showing cash inflows and outflows.
Statement of Position	Nonprofit financial report summarizing assets, liabilities, and net assets.
Tax Form 990	Standard IRS tax form for nonprofits.
Tax Form 990- EZ	IRS tax form for nonprofits, simpler than the 990.
Tax Form 990-N	IRS online tax form for small nonprofits, requesting basic information.
Tax Form 990-T	IRS tax form to report Unrelated Business Taxable Income.
Temporarily Restricted Net Asset	Net asset that accumulates donor-restricted revenues.
Unrestricted Net Asset	Net asset used for daily operations.

Index

CPSIA information can be obtained
at www.ICGtesting.com
Printed in the USA
LVHW060514170723
752627LV00004B/214

9 781505 995404